NINCOMP

NINCOMPOOPOLIS

The Follies of Boris Johnson

Douglas Murphy

Published by Repeater Books
An imprint of Watkins Media Ltd

19-21 Cecil Court
London
WC2N 4EZ
UK
www.repeaterbooks.com
A Repeater Books paperback original 2017
1

Printed and bound in the United Kingdom
Distributed in the United States by Random House, Inc., New York.

Cover design: Johnny Bull
Typography and typesetting: JCS Publishing Services Ltd
Typefaces: Chaparral Pro and Corbel

ISBN: 978-1-910924-57-0
Ebook ISBN: 978-1-910924-59-4

Contents

INTRODUCTION

"I'd like thousands of schools as good as the one I went to"

Boris Johnson, Mayor of London

Alexander Boris de Pfeffel Johnson, Alex to his family, Boris to the rest of us, was the Mayor of London from May 2008 to May 2016, a strange period that began in the throes of the global financial crisis and ended on the precipice of the UK's Brexit vote. It is no stretch to say that the man is polarising: to some he is "Boris the total legend", that rollicking bumbler with the ridiculous hair, a much-needed blast of fresh air blowing through the dank and fusty world of British politics. To others, however, he is the worst kind of upper-class twit — dangerous, ignorant, and in possession of a sense of entitlement straight out of the worst days of empire. In a very contemporary way he functions both as a politician and as an entertainment celebrity, in the British context and across the world: as Mayor of one of the world's major cities he became globally famous, an export symbol of English eccentricity, a cutaway tourist's facemask stacked in-between the Queen and David Beckham.

During his eight years in City Hall, there was crisis, disorder, and rioting, there were terror attacks, there was intrigue and corruption. But things didn't fall to pieces under his watch; in fact, it now looks like his period in power was a time of relative local stability in-between crises. The economy of London, massively dependent upon services and the City of London, weathered the storms, and if anything the imbalance between the successes of the capital and the rest of the UK became greater. Outsized wealth became more and more visible during this period, especially in the property market, but also in an upmarket transformation of London's leisure industry. Johnson's pro-business, pro-wealth message was one of the things that helped maintain London's reputation as a place to be easily rich, with the £100 million penthouses and £100 steaks to match.

But life didn't get better for most people during this time. The prime force making London life more difficult was housing, with the average cost of a home in London increasing by sixty percent in the eight years Johnson was in charge. But beyond that, cuts in benefits, funding for local authorities and other basic services, imposed by the Westminster government after 2010, made life harder for most of the people in the city. This was the era of "austerity", when we were told that the economy was like a cupboard that had been munched empty by the previous government, and that — most conveniently — anti-state cost-cutting was the only thing to be done. Some showboating objections aside, ideologically this was the world that Johnson believed in, and in which Londoners were forced to live.

The built environment of London changed rapidly during the Johnson years, with large volumes of output, most significantly in the private housing sector, but also major transport and infrastructure projects. Areas that had lain dormant for long periods finally saw the cranes arrive, such as the long-gestating Battersea Power Station project that finally began after three decades of failed schemes. Elsewhere, areas of public housing found themselves threatened in a way not seen since the early 1990s, as packs of developers sniffed around the unrealised value in comparatively low-density neighbourhoods of people too poor to afford obscene market rates.

These changes in the built environment were overseen by Johnson, but he had an impact on the form of London far more directly, for during his time at City Hall he conceived of and commissioned a number of projects that to all intents and purposes came directly from his own heart. Ranging from architecture to public art to transport, they rank amongst the stupidest, most ill-conceived works of design I've seen in my life, a series of whimsical follies stunning not only for the shallowness of their conception, but also for the sheer fact that the unstoppable will of Johnson managed to make so many of them happen.

Almost in homage to one of his beloved classical megalomaniacs, Johnson's interventions in the built environment are some of the most remarkably odd public works anywhere in the world in recent years, monuments to his lack of imagination, and this book is first and foremost about them. It tells the story of how they came to appear, the struggles against them, and the aftermath of their realisation. It is often a story of urban embarrassment, of the shame of having to watch as these objects appeared, but it is also a story of how this kind of personality could achieve such things in a world of faceless business, faceless bureaucracy, endless procurement and tendering processes. It suggests that with the right drive it is still possible to make big things happen, only that in this case it's a shame that the big things were such a bloody mess.

#

Whilst he is the primary focus, this book is not a warts-and-all portrait of Johnson, and it is not a behind-the-scenes look at the machinations of City Hall. There is no secret network of informants that have fed me the real stories behind events, although in most cases the goings-on have been fairly obvious — Johnson not being a man particularly good at keeping secrets. Furthermore, a number of journalists, both professional and amateur, tracked his movements from day one and their work has done us all a great service.

For many, Johnson will be a familiar character, but his back-story is worth recounting, because it shows not only the complexity of the man but also the strange division of the elite that he hails from, and what's more, it tragically helps to shed light on the interpersonal dynamics that have caused so much damage to the country in recent years.

The basic story that is told about Johnson is that he is ambition incarnate, that as a child he wanted to be "king of the world", and that he has never wavered from this desire. But for a man seen as such a distillation of "Englishness" he has a far more inflected and subtle background. He was born on 19th June 1964 in New York, as his father Stanley was at that point a postgrad at Columbia, studying economics. His mother Charlotte is an artist, and Johnson comes from that strange substrata of the ruling class, where underneath the titles and the land a current of bohemianism runs.

His father later worked for the World Bank and the EEC, with a focus on environmental issues, and Johnson spent his early years being shuttled around European schools, before being packed off to Eton. On the one hand it is worth noting that Johnson is not a "Shire Tory", coming from a more peripatetic and intellectual background, but his was undoubtedly an ultra-elite beginning, one which raises the intriguing question of whether a similar child would be able to experience that kind of start now, what with the massive rises in fees and the competition from the ultra-wealthy that threatens the clear access the old British elite once had to their educational privilege.

At Eton, Johnson was pals with Charles Spencer (Lady Diana's brother) and Darius Guppy, whose ancestor gave his name to the fish. Johnson was a King's Scholar, and won prizes in English and Classics, which highlights his oft-doubted intelligence, but this may well have been the high-point of his academic career. It is worthwhile noting the famous culture of popularity that is cultivated at Eton, with privileges often being dependent upon lobbying fellow students, and how that seems to create young men utterly convincing in their insincerity. After a gap year in Australia he went up to Oxford to read Classics at Balliol in 1983, part of a generation of students there at the same time who would go on to dominate British politics — former PM David Cameron, former leader of the Tories William Hague, and other long-term colleagues and rivals such as Michael Gove, Jeremy Hunt, and Nick Boles.

Famously, while at Oxford Johnson was a member of the Bullingdon Club, the long-running elite dinner society famed for its riotous behaviour. A group photograph of the club from around 1986, in their signature blue tails, became famous as it showed both Cameron and Johnson as pompous young ultra-elite men, condescension almost oozing from the page. The Bullingdon (and their chant of "BULLER! BULLER! BULLER!") is one of the most infamous examples of the performative disdain of the elite, and tales of their untouchable antics of smashing restaurants would become deeply ironic in the years of austerity. In recent years, I've heard of occasions where the police, on finding out that the chaos they've been called to deal with is the work of the young Bullingdon men, say, "There's nothing we can do, as they always pay for the damage".

The famous rivalry between Cameron and Johnson is said to have begun at this time. Johnson, charming, eccentric, and outgoing, read Classics, while the more conventional Cameron, his eyes directly on the prize, read PPE. Symbolically, after the exams Johnson left with an upper-second while Cameron achieved a double-first, an initial victory that would echo throughout their later years. Cameron would go almost directly to Parliament as a researcher while Johnson took the winding road through journalism.

The Johnson everyone knows now begins to come into focus. Through contacts he got himself a job at the *Times*, but was fired for fabricating a quote in an article. A move over to the *Daily Telegraph* followed, where he worked as a leader writer, becoming Brussels Correspondent. It has recently been noted with a bitter irony that despite his own background and wide-world sensibility, Johnson's columns on the EU for the *Telegraph* became one of the big influences on the Eurosceptic tendency that would later be the undoing of so much.[1] Johnson helped take the distrust of the EU idea away from being a cause of the Left — in particular the Bennites — and turn it into one of national sovereignty against the insidious grey bureaucracy of the continent.

Johnson made his way to Assistant Editor by the late '90s, becoming a noted columnist, before taking the job of editor of the *Spectator* in 1999, a post he held for six years, increasing its circulation but becoming rather controversial for a number of reasons, some to do with laxness, triviality, and flippancy, some more serious, which eventually led to his removal.

Johnson is often described as being dodgy, and a number of well-known incidents have been arraigned against him over the years. One example was the discovery of a recording of a 1995 telephone conversation between Johnson and his old friend Darius Guppy — a convicted fraudster, who has boasted about attacking journalists who have offended him — in which Johnson appeared to obsequiously agree to source the personal information of a journalist that Guppy intended to assault.[2]

And in contradiction to Johnson's seemingly open mind, much of the content of the *Spectator* during his editorship was highly controversial. He made references to "picaninnies" and "watermelon smiles" in an article that discussed the Queen's visits around the Commonwealth, and he was widely criticised for continuing to publish the writings of "Taki", the acerbic

7

society diarist whose columns are regularly filled with racist, anti-Semitic, and on occasion pro-fascist content. A leader in the *Spectator* after the butchering of Kenneth Bigley by Iraqi militants in 2004 mocked Liverpudlians for their sentimentality and addiction to grief, giving them an extra kicking by repeating various slanders on the Hillsborough survivors.

Johnson's personal life is also a source of much lurid anecdote. After a first society marriage to Allegra Mostyn-Owen ended in divorce in 1993, Johnson became widely known as a philanderer, with a number of admitted infidelities committed against his second wife Marina Wheeler. His affair with the columnist Petronella Wyatt was one of the reasons he was eventually removed from the *Spectator*, and in 2013 a court case quashed an injunction to withhold the existence of a child he'd fathered with the arts consultant Helen MacIntyre. Whilst a private life is a private life, Johnson's reputation testifies to what is often said about him, that there is no room for any kind of consideration for the personhood of others; that the world revolves around him.

The years of having his cake and eating it were still part of a long-term drive upwards. Despite their different levels of concentration, Johnson and Cameron both became MPs in 2001, part of a new generation of Tories entering the House of Commons at the party's lowest ebb after the rise of New Labour. Johnson's seat was Henley, which had previously been Michael Heseltine's. Johnson didn't rise anywhere near as quickly as Cameron, who — with Johnson's support — became leader of the Tories in 2005, at that point being seen as a younger, bluer version of the by-now discredited Tony Blair. But there was one thing more than any other that made Johnson a fixture in the public consciousness at this point, and this was the series of appearances from 1998 that he made on the satirical TV quiz show *Have I Got News for You*. As both panellist and then later guest host, Johnson entertained everyone as a stuttering, self-deprecating, eccentric toff, willing to sit there looking impishly bemused as everyone roared in laughter at his apparent lack of comprehension. He became an audience favourite, his name shortened to simply Boris, and his celebrity status was ensured.

As an MP, he was promoted under Cameron to being Shadow Secretary of State for Education, not exactly a top post, and Johnson was criticised for a lacklustre and non-committal effort in the Commons. He voted slightly to the left of the party, particularly on LGBT and other gender issues, and was considered popular in the Henley area, but he toed the cross-party line on the Iraq War. But with the long game in consideration, he had already become one of the most well-known and recognisable politicians in the country, long before the decision to run for London Mayor occurred to him.

#

In the 1990s, the lack of a central municipal authority was a remarkable thing regarding a city of the size and importance of London. The previous authority, the Greater London Council, had been abolished by the Thatcher government, as part of their crusade to destroy local government and the Left in general. By the late '80s the GLC had been tarnished with the title "Loony Left", as it leaned in stark opposition to the government of the time, committed as it was to spending on public services, and supporting anti-racist and anti-discrimination politics and social movements. The leader of the GLC in its last years was Ken Livingstone, who from County Hall — across the Thames from Parliament — mounted a defiant challenge to the anti-state headbangers in charge of the country, and the overwhelming screech of the right-wing press.

But when 1997 rolled along, one of the things that New Labour had promised for many years was to reinstate a centralised London authority, a system that would be called the Greater London Authority, consisting of a Mayor and an Assembly, whose creation was confirmed through a referendum in 1998. The elections were to take place in May 2000, and were widely expected, considering the general urban leanings of London, and the context in the country as a whole, to return a Labour candidate as Mayor. Livingstone wished to stand as the Labour candidate, but in a foreshadowing of the problems that would bedevil the party over a decade later, the election weighted votes heavily towards MPs. Livingstone had been at the far-left of the party even in the '80s, and with the New Labour movement at its peak, the party was now far to the right of where they had been, with no intention to revisit previous battles. Livingstone failed to pick up the candidacy, being defeated by Frank Dobson, but such was the local regard for Livingstone, however, that he was able to stand as an independent and win, beginning his victory speech: "As I was saying before I was so rudely interrupted fourteen years ago...". Livingstone became the Mayor of London

for the next eight years, winning another election —
this time with Labour's blessing — in 2004.

One of the primary responsibilities of the Mayor
and the Assembly was the planning process, and this
is one factor that Livingstone will be remembered
most for. When Labour came back to power there was
a strong sense that the Conservative government had
been distinctly suburban, willing to abandon the inner-
cities in favour of the periphery, frightened of the very
nature of urban living. But the new vision that was
taking hold over those in power was that of the "Urban
Renaissance", where British cities long in decline could
be regenerated, taking lessons from the best examples of
high-density urbanism — such as the centre of Barcelona
— and bringing them to the UK to encourage a more
cosmopolitan culture.

The main mind behind the Urban Renaissance
was Richard Rogers, later Lord Rogers of Riverside,
the architect who had built one of the boldest British
buildings of the late 20th century for Lloyds of London,
but was now making an impact as an urbanist and
activist within the corridors of power. Rogers — who
had designed the Millennium Dome — became a design
advisor for the GLA (resigning in 2009 after a failed
attempt to get along with Johnson), and his vision,
basically understood as the introduction of sustainable
infrastructure, high-density living, and sophisticated
cafe culture to British cities, was the defining urban
concept of the time.

A typical example of the Rogers-influenced Livingstone
attitude to urbanism was the "100 Public Spaces" plan,
which was, as the title suggests, a proposal to remake

and upgrade one hundred different public spaces across the capital, from a proposal to pedestrianise Parliament Square, to renovation works on open spaces in poorer neighbourhoods like Dalston. Although over the eight years it barely made its way into double figures, the ethos behind the plan is clear — the creation of walkable urban environments and a public realm that was intended to encourage a more civic life in the inner city.

But what will perhaps define Livingstone's attitude to the built environment was the Faustian pact that he set up with developers and finance. The original GLA London Plan, published in 2004, described two of its main aims as "strong, diverse long term economic growth", and "social inclusivity to give all Londoners the opportunity to share in London's future success". London was a different place than it had been in the 1980s, when a common Left position was to bemoan the high-rise results of the building boom of the '60s–'70s, and demand that communities played a central role in their own physical development. Now in the optimistic Blair years the mood was to come to an understanding with finance capitalism, where business would be allowed to act more or less as it pleased as long as something was given back. The interaction of the aims in the London Plan hinted at an urban strategy whereby intensive development was to be encouraged in certain locations, especially those served particularly well by transport hubs, while at the same time increasing demands for affordable housing and other such attempts at redistribution.

The result of this concern for encouraging development to maintain growth meant that during the boom years before 2008, the skyline of London began to rapidly change, as new skyscrapers and dense housing began to reappear. Tall office blocks had not been built in London since the 1980s, with the completion of One Canada Square at Canary Wharf in 1990 the last for a long time, while large-scale housing hadn't been attempted since the collapse of the welfare-state housing programme in the 1970s. All of a sudden, there was life in London construction, and the years of British architects leaving the country to get work in Hong Kong and the Far East were over, with London becoming once again a recognised leader in the design industries. This urban renaissance was significant, and overall beneficial to the city as a whole, but years later it would be seen as far too complacent with regard to letting the development industry have its own way, especially considering what would happen later.

#

In 2008, Livingstone decided to run again, but familiarity fatigue, not only with him but with Labour in general, not to mention the distress of the onset of the banking crisis, meant that it was always going to be a difficult one to win for him. Meanwhile, Johnson, who had apparently "uhm"-ed and "ah"-ed even more than was usual over the prospect, had won the candidacy through an open election.

The two campaigns were very different, and cut across party and thus class lines. Livingstone pointed to the long boom, the improvement in services, the coming Olympics, as well as his dignified handling of the 2005 terror attacks, as reasons why he could be trusted to continue. Johnson, on the other hand, claimed that crime was out of control and that Livingstone had been ignoring the needs of most Londoners in favour of looking mainly to the inner cities. And while Livingstone received most of his campaign funds from Labour sources such as the party and unions, Johnson was very much the business candidate, with a variety of hedge-funders and other money types backing his low-tax vision.

Johnson also had the benefit of wide backing in the media, not just because of the wide support for the Tories, but also through various personal connections and friendships. Veronica Wadley, who was Editor of the *Evening Standard*, the main London newspaper, was relentlessly anti-Livingstone in the run-up to the election, for which loyalty Johnson made her a Senior Advisor in 2012. Another media helper was Andrew Gilligan, the ex-BBC man who was behind the "sexed-up" dossier story that led to the death of Dr David Kelly. Gilligan worked for Wadley at the *Evening Standard* and was an important part of the long campaign against Livingstone, and in 2013 Johnson gave Gilligan the job of Cycling Commissioner for London. It's hard to overstate the extent to which Johnson's existence as a political figure relied on these sorts of connections in the right-wing press, promoting him, excusing him, and generally looking after his interests, as he did theirs.

The 2008 campaign was also one of the first outings in the UK for the Australian electoral strategist Lynton Crosby, who encouraged Johnson not to attempt to win over urban voters, but to persuade the suburbanites to bother to come out and vote for him. Some of the things promised by Johnson included removing the western wing of the "congestion charge" zone (an area of Central London upon which a one-off charge is levied for entering, which Livingstone was expanding to include wealthy neighbourhoods such as Kensington and Chelsea), removing a proposed increase on charges for 4x4 vehicles, ending an oil supply deal that Livingstone had struck with the Chavez government of Venezuela, and abolishing the newsletters that Livingstone had issued to households, which Johnson called "council Pravdas". Another typically conservative move was the proposal to introduce a ban on drinking on public transport, as part of Johnson's crime-focussed campaign.

Sure enough, Johnson won the election on an increased turnout, and a significant step in the end of New Labour had begun. But what would Johnson as Mayor mean for the capital? Would there be any significant change in life there? Would the city look any different? How would he deal with the unravelling financial crisis? Would he be bothered enough to turn up?

FOLLIES

"A fantastic new landmark for London"

The Crystal

2008 was easily one of the worst years of my life. I had finished my postgraduate studies that summer, right as the financial crisis was at its height. The prospects for a trained but unqualified architect at this point had fallen off a cliff — projects were being cancelled left, right, and centre, nearly every firm was laying off staff, the entire industry was in turmoil. The year before, graduating students had woken up the morning after their degree show with a hangover and numerous job offers, and I had heard the phrase "bought off the wall" being crudely transposed from artists to architects. But without any real insider contacts, no amount of CV distribution could help me find a job, and so I found myself — after six years of study and training — collecting Job Seeker's Allowance in the job centre in Hoxton.

Considering what has been the case for the UK since then, the situation at that point was almost relaxed — the job centre was suddenly filled with twenty-somethings from the creative professions: architecture, design, fashion, film, and TV, etc., and there was little sign of the hyper-aggressive sanctioning that has now become normal. It wasn't quite relaxed however — the influx of temporarily embarrassed young adults didn't mask the general and consistent misery of the place, and even with the deterioration since, the previous decade had seen the introduction of a great deal of punitive measures against those out of work. Nevertheless, the extraordinary circumstances were palpable, and the eye-roll of the staff member hearing yet another new claimant sheepishly mumble "architect" was telling.

This humiliating state of affairs dragged on, so that by the end of 2009, more than a year later, I was still barely scraping by. Via contacts I had made while blogging about architecture, I had managed to start working as a journalist, and there were occasional scraps of freelance work here and there generating 3D images of luxury houses designed for wealthy Russians in the forests outside Moscow. It was enough to be no longer claiming benefits, but money was a constant worry and my lifestyle was Spartan. But then, not long after the beginning of 2010, a call came through from a university friend who had recently found a job — was I busy? There was a competition, the first sniff of new work for ages, and they needed people right away. I was in no position to refuse.

A few days later I turned up to an office that was situated in a converted warehouse building in the hinterland between Shoreditch and the City of London, and sat down to be given an introduction to the project. The site was a patch of derelict land at the side of the Royal Victoria Dock in East London that had once been the site of a warehouse, long since demolished. To the north was Canning Town, a residential neighbourhood where the Freemason's Estate once stood, the cluster of tower blocks that included Ronan Point, whose partial collapse in 1968 irrevocably soured the UK's relationship with prefabricated construction. This neighbourhood, to this day highly deprived, was and is separated from the docks by a long thread of railway lines.

In the years since the dereliction of the dockside, the Docklands Light Railway had been built to pass through, its automated carriages heading off to London City Airport, with its aura of executive travel and its thrilling flight paths over Canary Wharf. The locks that granted access to the docks had been filled in, with the waters barely disturbed except by the occasional use of the equipment at a watersports centre. Nearby the gigantic Excel Centre, one of the largest exhibition and trade-fair venues in Europe, had been completed in 2000.

On the immediate docksides, some areas to the south had been gradually redeveloped as low-rise housing, set back behind rows of Stothert and Pitt cranes, legacies of a time when the pressures of residential development were not quite so overwhelming. Not far away was the derelict hulk of the Millennium Mills, a mouldering fragment of the once overwhelmingly industrial docks, while directly to the north was a pumping station designed by Richard Rogers in the late 1980s. This small industrial building, overly designed with a polychromatic metal crown, was now overlooked by some faceless early-2000s flats, a plethora of cladding materials, none of them in any way convincing.

The brief for the new building that was to take its place there was, well, not immediately clear. It was to be some kind of exhibition or conference space, but the Excel Centre around the corner had more space like that available than you could ever need. There was an idea that there might be some kind of office required, but the building certainly wasn't to be a conventional office block, and the location was miles away from any of the centres of demand for office space. Overall, the brief, such as it was, said that the building had to be "sustainable", which wasn't exactly helpful for anyone figuring out what to design.

I rolled up my sleeves, got involved, and gradually the instructions coalesced. The building had a tenant in mind — Siemens — who had agreed to take on space for conferences and training. They had been tempted by the prospect of using the project as a showcase of their ongoing work in low-carbon energy and infrastructure. As a result, much of the building was to be given over to a permanent exhibition on sustainability. Exhibition designers hadn't been brought on at this point, so the competition entry developed as a big shed, folded and faceted to make an iconic form, but with a huge internal space, big enough to hold the world's then-largest wind-turbine blades, which were seen as the sort of spectacular objects that might well feature as part of the exhibition.

It seemed, from what could be gathered, that this competition was an idea developed by Johnson, who was looking for opportunities to kick-start the redevelopment of the remaining derelict areas beside the docks. He had apparently managed to talk Siemens into the project, which would be a joint venture with the London Development Agency, with the promise that it would be complete in time for the 2012 Olympics, with, presumably, the opportunity to use the building for promotional activities during this time. There was clearly a strong political momentum behind the project, but it didn't seem all that clear that anyone knew what it was actually for.

Eventually, the competition was won by the collaborative team of two architecture firms that I had assisted, although I played no further part in the project beyond that point. The scheme that went into planning in mid-2010, and was completed only a short time after the Olympics, described itself as an "urban sustainability centre". The original big folded shed idea had been reduced in scope, but had now been rationalised as being derived from crystalline forms, with the entire development being christened as "The Crystal". One half of the building was to be given over to a large auditorium and surrounding office space, while the other half was the aforementioned sustainability exhibition. The whole building was to be an exemplar

The Crystal - 'Iconic' regeneration, speculative housing, spectacular infrastructure. Johnson's London. (Image author's own).

of low-carbon technologies, including photovoltaics, recycled construction materials, rainwater harvesting and the like, with the intention that it would be the most advanced building of this type in the UK.

The result sits rather incongruously in its landscape, but is a perfectly acceptable building, with a certain charm to its folds and facets, wilful though they are. But The Crystal is certainly not one to take its place in the list of major London attractions, and apart from one major example it didn't encourage much new development in its surroundings. But in many ways this slightly purposeless architectural object, in whose production I played a small part, is a perfect example of what I would come to understand as Johnson's attitude to the built environment. A large source of investment — whether an institution or an individual — would be encouraged to put money into a project for which there was no real need, in exchange for branding and promotional opportunities. This funding would be topped up by the public purse, without any significant oversight. The new project would be portrayed as a vital part of maintaining London's position as a global city, with any opposition condemned as hopeless negativity, even if the object ended up making London into a laughing stock.

The Crystal, despite its cringe-worthy name, has suffered no major humiliations since its construction, instead just sitting puzzlingly at the side of the docks. To its north, a forlorn-looking derelict pub has been demolished, and some more speculative flats, their cylindrical forms decorated by waving ribs of balconies, are, at the time of writing, almost finished. But this muted acceptance is not the case for every Johnsonian project that has been foisted upon the city and its landscape. Some of them have been damp squibs, others are innocuous enough, but some are affronts to urbanism, attempts to infantilise the landscape to the point of incoherence.

"It would have boggled the minds of the Romans"

The ArcelorMittal Orbit

When the crisis hit I had been living in London for a few years, first moving down in the summer of 2005 after finishing my undergraduate degree. I had a job waiting for me at an architect's office in Shoreditch, in yet another converted old warehouse building from the early 20th century. Not knowing what to do about living, I had taken an A–Z and drawn a circle depicting a half-hour's walk from my new workplace, which determined where I wanted to live. Using "Loot", the London listings paper, and "Moveflat", a then-popular website for room lettings, I found a room in an ex-council flat in Shadwell, an area of East London traditionally tied to the docks. In the decades since containerisation moved the port downstream, Shadwell had declined, and was by then one of the most deprived parts of London, with a patchwork landscape of estates and older housing largely defined by the destruction left by the Luftwaffe.

The room had a small circular sticker in the corner of the window, already faded from the sun: "BACK THE BID", it said. When I arrived, it was the week after the 7th July tube and bus bombings in London, and the whole city was on edge. The tragedy and horror of the attacks, and their grim inevitability during the height of the "war on terror", completely overshadowed what had happened only the day before, when the IOC had awarded the 2012 Olympic Games to London.

The madness surrounding the bombings went on for weeks, not least when another set of bombers attempted identical attacks two weeks later, followed the next day by the mistaken-identity police killing of Jean Charles de Menezes. There were constant alerts, and my hunt for a room had involved numerous disrupted journeys as the underground was evacuated yet again after a bomb scare. I indulged a little in strange magical behaviours — only getting on at the very ends of trains, thinking the middle carriages were a more obvious target, for example — and in one surreal and disturbing incident I saw a tube worker and a policeman, nerves completely frayed, getting into a fist fight in front of an emptied Kings Cross Station.

But gradually, as time went on, the bombings began to fade into memory, and the normal London routine set in again. This is, of course, the dynamic of how terrorism and the response to it works — in sophisticated urban scenes it is practically impossible to stop low-complexity violent attacks, and the only basic practical response is to maintain normal functions and habits. The response of ordinary Londoners to those events was in many ways exemplary, in part fashioned by the long years of the Irish Troubles, which at some points during the early 1990s involved bomb attacks almost weekly.

In fact, it was the events of 6th July 2005 that were to become far more a part of the day-to-day life of the city in the years to come — the question of the Olympics, and the massive transformation of East London that they were due to effect, gradually became part of the ambient London hum. I left the Shadwell flat years before the

Olympics took place, but while I was there, that sticker was a constant little reminder of what was going on in the background.

The proposals for the Olympics went through phases and developments. Beijing was to host the games in 2008, and it was clear the Chinese were intending to go all out on a display of their new-found prowess.

Having to follow that example, based as it was upon the euphoria of mass urbanisation and years of double-digit economic growth, not to mention experience of massive amounts of highly planned public works, was never going to be easy, even before the onset of the financial crisis. An early masterplan for the London site, the valley of the River Lea as it passed between Hackney and Stratford, worked on by the now-defunct Foreign Office Architects, showed swoops and flourishes crawling across the site in a digital animation. This attempt at some kind of experimental landscape was typical of the self-proclaimed radical fringes of architecture in the early 2000s, designed by an avant-garde architect whose Shoreditch office stood directly across from *Vice* magazine's pub the Old Blue Last, but little of this initial approach found its way into later designs.

Johnson's attendance at the Beijing ceremony, one of his first major mayoral outings, included some of his quintessentially half-informed monologues (such as his lecture to the Chinese about the real origin of table tennis being an English game called "Whiff Whaff")[3], but by and large, he was slow to assert his authority on the development of the Olympics themselves. By the time that "austerity" had been asserted as a dominant political concept for the coming years, the Olympics were ready to play their role in asserting that story — the London Games would not be profligate, nor wasteful, they would not fall into the trap of constructing boondoggles that no one would subsequently use. Instead, the Olympics were to be focussed on sustainability and "Legacy", on the creation of a functioning, integrated new neighbourhood and facilities that would seamlessly become part of the London fabric.

The designs developed for the three main venues reflected these ideals to differing degrees. The athletics stadium, rather than the bombastic "Bird's Nest" of steel from Beijing, was considered more as a temporary construction, and was designed (by HOK Sport, now known as Populous) as an adaptable and lightweight affair, to be converted cheaply into a football stadium afterwards. Hopkins Architects were commissioned to design the Velodrome, whose cable-net roof also subscribed to the logic of efficient steel construction. However, this minimal, "flat-pack" approach was somewhat undermined by Zaha Hadid Architects gaining the commission for the Aquatics Centre, wherein they used their computers to generate a sweeping formalist swoosh performing an impression of a marine animal, whose headachingly complex structure weighed ten times as much as the cycling venue's.[4]

By the time work on the Olympics began, the area around the Lea Valley had long become a somewhat forgotten zone. The Stratford Works railway depot had been there since the late 19th century, but the area along the Lea River had remained undeveloped right into the 20th. Gradually it became a "liminal" zone, home to factories and warehouses and other light-industrial uses, but generally unvisited by the wider population. The Abercrombie Plan of 1944 envisaged the Lea Valley as part of a linear park reaching all the way down to the Thames, a proposal whose long-delayed realisation was part of the pitch for the redevelopment of the Olympic site.

The area also played a small role in architectural history when at a point in the late 1960s it was to have been the location of Joan Littlewood & Cedric Price's project for a "Fun Palace", an interactive entertainment venue, something like a proto-Pompidou Centre, that is one of the great unrealised 20th-century architectural projects. This particular legacy would exert a gentle influence on the Olympic Stadium itself, as Peter Cook, once a member of architectural provocateurs Archigram (for whom Price was a primary influence), was enlisted to bring some of this cybernetic magic to the design of the stadium itself.

By the end of the century, the Lea Valley and surroundings were becoming known, however partially, as sites of imaginative reconstruction — Hackney Wick nearby was home to a growing live/work population of artists, and figures involved in "London Psychogeography", exemplified by the author Iain Sinclair, were known to explore its overgrown landscapes of canals, factories, pylons, ruins and other such melancholy sights, such as the famous "fridge mountain" made up entirely of discarded white goods[5]. A booming property market, alongside estate demolition and legal restrictions on squatting, meant that many neighbourhoods of the city were becoming far more prosaic than they had been in the 1980s, and the Lea Valley, with its associations with rave culture and

The Olympic Village - Britain's showcase attempt at housing achieves a basic continental European standard, although too windswept for some. (Image author's own).

other subversive activities, was one of the last places where a certain sense of marginal, experimental London clung on.

Approaching the Olympic site now from Stratford, nearly a decade after the first decontamination works began and nearly five years after the event itself, it has become a new part of the city better than many people expected. The Westfield shopping centre, with its infamous ruse of forcing those accessing the Olympic Park to travel through its malls, is thriving, while the 1970s Stratford Centre that it usurped remains half-hidden behind some flimsily expensive aluminium leaves, commissioned to hide the reality of Stratford from visiting eyes.

To the north, the Olympic Village itself, supposedly a showcase of the very best of British housing architecture but actually more like a run-of-the-mill continental suburban development, is bedding in, the large-perimeter blocks presenting a fairly dignified front to their surroundings. This safe mediocrity isn't consistent however, with some genuinely upsetting student housing and a developer's gold-rush of tacky towers to the outskirts of the park very much spoiling the architectural mood.

From the west, the park is entered through Hackney Wick, an area that has undergone remarkable change in recent years. An urban mess largely made up of warehouse and factory buildings, it was to most Londoners for much of the late 20th century just the end of the bus route, a grimy landscape bounded by canals and severed from Hackney proper by the thundering A12 Blackwall Tunnel approach road. In 1985, the neighbourhood produced one of the iconic images of London's decline when the botched demolition of one of the seven point blocks of the Trowbridge Estate — one of the most notorious housing developments of the 1960s — left most of the building intact, a humiliating sight known as "The Leaning Tower of Hackney".

By the time I was living in London, Hackney Wick was known as a party hotspot. Landlords had turned large industrial buildings into studios, which in turn had often been turned into ultra-cheap flats, creating a highly communal environment often contained within single buildings. Some of the conversions were beautiful in a bohemian-garret way, with vast volumes of unheated space enlivened by the paraphernalia of art production, their Spartan industrial materials softened by plants and domestic furniture, while others were horrible dungeons fit only for decadence, of which there was plenty to be found, albeit of a fairly conventional sort.

Gradually, this odd state of affairs became normalised. Hipster enterprises opened up in what had been greasy spoons for industrial workers, some residents stayed on and started families, and Hackney Council commissioned intelligent and creative landscaping from Muf Architecture/Art. Some of the warehouses were demolished to make way for nondescript speculative housing, whose corridor-less interiors billed themselves as "warehouse-style". But the Olympics sent the process into overdrive, with the prospect of the area no longer being the forgotten eastern fringe of Hackney, but henceforth becoming the western edge of the new Olympic Park.

A trip through Hackney Wick now passes by many of the old warehouse buildings, their unornamented brick

Hackney Wick, pre Olympics - Warehouses, graffiti, regeneration, and in the distance, spectacle. (Image author's own).

covered in street art, that peculiar character of light-industrial urbanism transposed into residential use, but the appearance of more money washing through is palpable. Political anti-gentrification graffiti is visible everywhere, while "characterful" bars and restaurants have been brought in as landlords realise what it is that they actually possess. More recently, the long-delayed and somewhat controversial re-occupation of the Olympic Stadium by West Ham United has meant that Saturdays see a huge influx of football fans, a social demographic that hadn't used the area much since it moved from material to cultural production a generation ago.

Hackney Wick has become busy and bustling in a way it hadn't been for a long time, its eerie quiet now mostly a thing of the past, and it is due to be altered yet further, as

Queen Elizabeth Olympic Park - Post-liminal cultivated wildness, gradually encircled by towers. (Image author's own).

many more of the studio buildings are being swept aside for post-Olympic redevelopment. From Hackney Wick Station, exiting past the Lord Napier, an occasionally-squatted derelict pub totally coated in graffiti, past the demolished ruins of a large factory building that for years stood proudly demonstrating its "Mr Bagel's" signage, complete with grocer's apostrophe, one can walk up White Post Lane towards the park. The street threads through warehouses, bars, theatres, restaurants, and galleries, before crossing the Hackney Cut canal and entering a completely different form of space.

Once across the water, everything is new. The ground is new, the paving is new, the signage is new. The grass and plants, arranged in the still-just-about-fashionable "wild meadow" style, are fresh and young. The canals and rivers, once filled with detritus, fetid and dank from years of neglect, are clean and softly edged — while large patches of the park have been given over to aesthetically pleasing marsh for flood protection. Some materials aren't doing so well — there is a pale beige walking surface that was already decaying very soon after the park opened, but generally speaking the surroundings are very pleasant, with the occasional retained memento from their previous condition, and on warm clear days it is well used by people from all surrounding neighbourhoods.

The athletics stadium has re-opened, but not without a number of scandals relating to the costs and the contracts of converting it to football use, with the tendering process having to be re-run due to legal challenges. The design may have been light and supposedly demountable, an attempt to plug into a history of British avant-gardism in

Zaha Hadid Architects - Aquatics Centre. Structure, construction and labour visually minimised in the service of metaphoric formal gesture. (Image author's own).

technological architecture, but it was not a simple task to prepare it for its new use, in many ways a telling example of the gap between the rhetoric of architectural flexibility and its actual implementation.

Further towards Stratford, the Aquatics Centre cuts an undeniably impressive figure. Its allusive form conjures up various watery connotations — whales, rays, waves, or perhaps a Muybridge-style time-lapse of a swimmer in action. Like much digitally-designed architecture, it looks better viewed from an angle, its twisting qualities tending to vanish when seen straight on. The pool itself is municipally run, and features some surprisingly good concrete detailing from the studio of Zaha Hadid, who are still not known for their strong attention to the close-up experience of architecture. During the Olympics it was disappointing that the charismatic formalism of the building was hidden by huge temporary bleachers, and the building recently had to have darkening film applied to its huge windows in order to cut out the glare, but it will probably be known as one of the best buildings that Hadid — who died suddenly in March 2016 — ever completed.

In recent years, a certain type of article has become popular online, one which revisits former Olympic sites that have been abandoned. This particular branch of the "ruin porn" aesthetic takes pleasure in the diminishment of these spaces of pageantry, alluding to classical antiquity in its leching over spoiled concrete, grassed-up flame cauldrons and crumbling rings, with the rapidly diminished remains of Athens 2004 being particular favourites. Compared to this, then, the legacy of the London Olympics has been a remarkable success, and despite a few terrible-quality high-rise buildings appearing at the fringes, it is of remarkably consistent experiential and visual quality.

Apart from one thing.

#

It can't be missed. It can't be ignored.

It looms over the whole park, you can hardly get out of its sight. Further away, it ruins your mood when it appears framed by the vanishing point along Roman Road; it peeks menacingly over the trees and roofs across much of East London. It is a constant reminder of Johnson, and his maddening inability to leave things alone.

But what even is it? It's red, that's for sure, a putrid, raw, bloody red, and it's illuminated at night by red-

37

tinted spotlights, in case the colour might escape you in the darkness. It's hollow, a metallic frame, something like a radio mast or construction crane, but it appears to be trying to be a surface, a swirling, rotated tube, a frozen instant of some wet creature flaring and thrashing around in the air. It has no symmetry, it doesn't reach a point at the top and it doesn't seem to rest easily on the ground, it is not poised, rather it is arrested.

If you can bear to keep looking at it, you see that within the whorls of the edifice is a vertical structure, carrying lifts that lead up to a disc-shaped building resting inside the steel vortex. The difference in register is hilarious — the cheap panelling of this platform, set within the lurid tangle of the structure itself, is like a small roadside office block, the home of a car-clamping service, perhaps, set within the mouth of some infernal worm. Leading down around the lift shaft is a slowly spiralling structure with perforated sides, a staircase that leads back to the ground, further complicating the whole broken ensemble.

Approaching this cacophony of forms, some kind of constructional logic becomes apparent. The whole thing is largely made from tubular steel, welded into six-pointed star-like elements, which have then been bolted together. This form triangulates the structure, heavier and denser towards the bottom, lighter and more reduced towards the top. The loops that twirl around actually appear concertina-like, as the triangles fold in and out in order to join everything together properly, negating the illusion of smoothness that it appears to aim for.

Attending more closely, the structure appears to flare out like a trumpet at the bottom, and in a dark counterpart to its service-station-ish loft, a huge rusted steel bell is suspended just above the ground within it. For a number of years this unresolved tangle seemed fixed, but recent works to the site have left a further metallic structure snaking its way down and around the angular red twists. This tube swirls around smoothly, lightly twirling around the arms of the giant, adding yet more confusion to the overall mess but perhaps having a certain grace to its forms.

Any attempts to get close to the structure bring you right up against a security fence, holding you back almost as if the thing behind were a radio listening post or some other Cold War military site, officially non-existent but plain as day for all to see. The only way in is through a small pavilion of corporate appearance, and entrance is ticketed, restricted. This thing, this tremendous mess, is an attraction.

The Orbit Rises - Unintended formal resonances occur when viewed from the wrong side of the tracks. (Image author's own).

It is called the Orbit, or to give it its full name, the ArcelorMittal Orbit. It was not part of the original Olympic bid, nor part of the masterplan. Its existence is almost entirely down to the efforts of Johnson, who conceived of the project, and muscled it into existence through sheer gusto and opportunism. Again, there was no demand for it to exist, and it's not entirely clear what it does — at various points it has been described as an artwork, a viewing platform, a visitor attraction, a hire space, and now an extreme entertainment venue, offering, as it does, abseiling and a giant — indeed, "the world's longest"[6] — slide. It has not been a financial, popular, or critical success, and quite clearly it undermines the positive qualities of the rest of the Olympic site.

The Orbit has involved a number of people who are considered to be at the apex of their fields. It was designed by Anish Kapoor, one of the world's most successful sculptors and public artists, and was engineered by Cecil Balmond, one of the few structural engineers to carry some kind of celebrity outside of his field. It now incorporates a work by Carsten Höller, another of the art world's superstars. Yet these people have found their names attached to a ridiculous, pointless object that shows none of their talents in a good light, even if it may well have been profitable for them personally. But while the design may be attributed to these luminaries, and although the entire project may have been Johnson's brainchild, it required a chance encounter with one extra special man to make the Orbit happen at all.

#

In the years leading up to the Olympics, the richest man in Britain was Lakshmi Mittal. Born in India in 1950, his father ran and then owned a large steel business, into which the young Mittal directly moved. After a split from the family business in the 1990s, Mittal set up his own company, and through mergers and acquisitions it grew to become ArcelorMittal, since 2006 the largest steel company in the world. The vicissitudes of the global commodities market have meant that his decade-long stint as the UK's number-one richest man is now over, but his worth is still measured in the tens of billions of dollars.

Mittal has lived in the UK since the 1990s, one of the increasingly infamous ultra-high-net-worth individuals (UHNWIs) who have settled in London over the years, taking advantage of its political stability, its always-increasing property prices, as well as its accommodation of super-luxurious lifestyles. He is known to own three separate properties on Kensington Palace Gardens, a quintessentially leafy West London street that leads between Notting Hill Gate and Kensington Road, home to many embassies (including the ultra-secure Israeli embassy), and with guard posts continually manned by heavily armed police at either end. One of these properties, bought by Mittal in 2004 for £67 million, was at the time the most expensive house in the world.

Like most billionaires, Mittal is not a figure immune to controversy. He is known for buying up dilapidated and declining steel works in his search for latent value, and perhaps partly as a result of this strategy, safety, slave labour, and pollution scandals have followed him through his career. Further, it is perhaps only natural that as part of the cut and thrust of mergers and acquisitions, he would occasionally be associated with bribery scandals. Indeed, in his early years in the UK, a £125,000 donation he made to the Labour Party became controversial after it turned out that Tony Blair subsequently recommended Mittal's company to the Romanian government, hinting that the privatisation of their national steel industry and sale to Mittal might help them gain entry to the EU. This became known as the "Cash for Influence" scandal, and was in some ways typical of the kind of dirt that was dug up on New Labour, before the catastrophe of the Iraq War.[7]

But this is not to say that Mittal is particularly different from any other billionaire in terms of morals. And indeed, like many capitalists, what he takes with one hand he gives back with the other, and he is a large and grand contributor to a great many charitable schemes, including a donation that paid for a children's facility at Great Ormond Street Hospital in London. One of his particular charitable interests is sport, including a foundation he set up to support the training of Indian athletes for the Olympic Games.

The exact details regarding his encounter with Johnson are unclear, with the various details of the story actually told admitting interpretations ranging from a friendly encounter in a hotel lobby to a cordial chat whilst stood pissing into adjacent urinals. Whatever the details, it seems that Johnson was in Davos for the World Economic Forum in 2009, at which point he spotted Mittal, whom he quickly cornered and spouted forth his plans to adorn the Olympics with something extra special. The only problem was that he couldn't really spend all that money out of the public purse, so would Mr Steel perhaps be interested?

Recounting the story later, Johnson claimed that Mittal there and then agreed to provide the steel for what would later become the Orbit. And of course it all makes sense — Johnson clearly had an idea to add something to the Games, and a close personal exchange with someone who had not only gigantic wealth but also an interest in sport, and who would stand to benefit from being associated with such an object, considering the billions of eyes that would be on London for the event, was a fantastic intervention.

If it's to be believed, it's a good old risk-taking capitalist adventure, the little London guy meeting the big Steel guy, and through the little guy displaying enough balls they both get what they want. It almost makes you wonder what could be achieved if that energy and guile were put towards something actually useful.

#

Johnson's origin myth for the Orbit makes clear that by as early as 2009 he had decided that something extra had to be added to the Games to make them more interesting. As much of the outline masterplanning was already complete by the time that Johnson became Mayor, this must have been one of his first interventions into the process. He would later describe how "we felt that it really needed something extra — it needed a landmark".[8] On the one hand this completely went against the "austerity" conception of the Games, but on the other it could conceivably be slotted into the idea of "legacy", of something memorable that would make the Games stand out.

Johnson continued: "So I thought what do other people do when they have a fantastic world expo, or Olympic Games or a world fair? They have some kind of structure that people want to take their kids up to and look down from. So that was the idea." Again, if we take this statement at face value, Johnson is displaying a slight but perhaps rather shallow understanding of the built cultures of Expos and the Olympics. Yes, there are towers, such as the Eiffel Tower from the 1889 Paris Expo, or the Space Needle from the 1962 Seattle Expo, and yes, the Olympics have generated towers such as the one from Munich 1972, but he could just as easily have thought about legacies such as Flushing Meadows Park, left over from the 1964 NY World's Fair, or indeed, as he would later consider in different circumstances, the Crystal Palace of 1851.

But with this vision pulsing in his head, Johnson took whatever opportunities came along to push forward with this idea of a vertical icon for the Olympics. And with the promise of money and steel from Mittal, he was able to drive the idea directly towards its realisation.

The first that the public heard of the Orbit was in late 2009 when the announcement was seeded into the press that a tower was to be constructed as part of the Games. An early visual concept that was circulated was an image made by artist Paul Fryer entitled "Transmission", which appeared to be something like a giant electricity pylon, but in the context of an art object conceived as something monumental, perhaps ceremonial. While this idea placed the concept in the public eye, a giant pylon clearly was not going to be anywhere near spectacular enough, and a further competition was held to determine the design of the tower.

The jury was made up of various luminaries from the London art scene, including Nicholas Serota of the Tate, Julia Peyton-Jones and Hans Ulrich Obrist of the Serpentine Gallery, and Anita Zabludowicz of the eponymous art collection. The three shortlisted entries were the Kapoor/Balmond design, an entry from Antony Gormley, and a third submission from architects Caruso St John. A sketch from the back of a name tag from an awards ceremony[9] suggest that Caruso St John's entry was a tripartite, slightly classical, early New York skyscraper-ish structure, whereas Gormley — to no great surprise — proposed a giant naked human form, presumably his.

The project was launched in October 2010 with a press conference, which produced a memorable image of Johnson, Kapoor, Mittal, Balmond, and Tessa Jowell, grins frozen as they posed for pictures behind a large model of the Orbit. Other images that were sent out to the public that day showed widely skewed digitally-generated perspectives of the structure surrounded by thousands of tiny ant people, its steel rendered as a shimmeringly reflective polished material that made the design seem even less believable.

At the launch, Johnson predictably kept the tone low by calling the project the "Hubble Bubble", because he claimed it reminded him of a shisha pipe. In his defence, he probably only saw it that morning and may well have been on the Edgware Road recently before. But the descriptions from the designers themselves were barely any better. A planning document released to go with the design explained that they believed that:

> It should make an iconic statement about 'Tower-ness'. They looked at epoch making towers such as the Eiffel, Tatlin, Empire State and even the Pyramids. They could see that all conventional or classical structures want to accumulate strength and are thus stable ground based structures. Furthermore all towers are continuous in the vertical plane. This was a premise which Kapoor and Balmond wished to unravel and to destabilise.[10]

This was lazy bunkum, half-baked public-art rhetoric that should have been beneath people supposedly at the top of their game. The nods to some kind of deconstructive technique, the idea that through twisting and folding the structure, making its structural performance unclear, they were somehow challenging and subverting the notion of "towerness", is truly inane. The allusions were useless too, not only to the Eiffel Tower, which was far more than twice the height, and for forty years the tallest artificial structure in the world, a genuinely epochal construction, but also to Tatlin's Monument to the Third International, superficially similar but worlds away in spirit, an unbuilt dialectical giant that will forever remain a utopian ghost haunting the worlds of art and architecture.

Indeed, with a little detective work and intuition, it seems reasonable to reconstruct how the design came to be. It's probable that the competition invitation landed very late, and had to be worked on extremely quickly. There would have been some phone calls to set up a collaboration, followed by a meeting or two during which some sketches would have been produced by Kapoor, probably depicting something vaguely similar to the end result. This would then have been taken as the basis of a CAD model, where a single looped surface would have been divided up into a faceted tubular structure. For practical reasons the structure itself was effectively treated as a tripod — away from the main tower two loops come down to touch the ground and thus anchor the whole thing, while the lopsidedness of the viewing platform is offset by the sheer mass of other loops facing the other direction.

Digital analysis of the inherent loads in the structure would have meant that various tweaks would have been made to the form, both to make it stable but also to avoid excess deflection and other problems, but the engineers would also have had the thickness of the pipes themselves to manipulate for this purpose. It's worth noting that despite both the rhetoric and the visual appearance of destabilised curves flowing around in loops, the Orbit is effectively a vertical tower (containing the lift shaft) from which various objects lean outwards, which overall manages to maintain its balance.

It's tempting to feel sorry for Kapoor in all this, as the Orbit appears to take some of the themes from his previous work — like his Tate Modern sculpture Marsyas, on which he collaborated with Balmond — such as the stretched surfaces, blood-red colouring, expressionist forms, and massive scale, but then has created a kind of digitally-distorted bargain-basement version of them. The rusty bell that sits at the bottom is almost like a separate artwork in itself, as if Kapoor only managed to take control of a small part of the process. But in fact Kapoor is just as responsible for the overall object as anyone else, and perhaps should have been more careful about letting himself get caught up in such an ill-formed creative process.

During the run-up to the Olympics, as the park was being transformed, it was all hidden away behind hoardings, and was in fact difficult to see. One possible vantage point was from the Greenway, which is a linear park set upon an earthwork running along the Northern Outfall Sewer, one of Bazalgette's great works in the early Victorian years, bringing modern sanitation to the world's largest city after numerous outbreaks of

The Olympic Site - For years, the works were only visible as a snatched view from the train. (Image author's own).

cholera and other diseases. The Greenway was once a quintessential part of liminal East London, leading nowhere in particular, not exactly very green, and offering views mostly of the crinkly tin roofs of warehouses. Indeed, before the Olympics one of its most common associations was as a graveyard for burnt-out joyridden cars. But during the Olympic construction, it became one of the only places from which the construction could be seen, with a temporary viewing platform positioned to stare out at the sea of mud. On a few occasions before the Olympics I took foreign students on walks that passed along the Greenway, attempting to juxtapose in their minds the disorder of post-industrial London with the massive redevelopment then ongoing.

But there were even better views to be had. Even as the park was being moulded, trains still had to run through to the sprawling Stratford station, which brings together underground, overground, "Docklands Light", and continental High-Speed railways. Throughout this period I had a weekly job at a magazine whose offices were in Epping, at the far end of the Central Line in Essex. Taking a train from Hackney Central to Stratford on the Overground Line, which had been upgraded in 2007 before Johnson took office, involved travelling straight through the centre of the Olympic Park, under the stadium, right past the Aquatics Centre, and then, gradually, under the rapidly rising construction of the Orbit.

I genuinely couldn't quite believe it was happening; that something so tossed-off, with so little thought put into it, was being assembled in front of my eyes. I would turn and press my nose to the glass, aghast, watching as each of the steel starfishes was hoisted into place, with a

couple of men on harnesses bolting the pieces together.
I felt perhaps a little like the character in the apocalyptic
BBC TV film *Threads*, who, upon climbing out from under
a parked flatbed truck, sees a nuclear mushroom cloud
billowing out above Sheffield, and can only say "They've
done it... They've bloody done it!"

#

The Olympics came and went, and in fact I barely noticed
them. I was quite ill while they happened, and so missed
much of the excitement through being concerned more
with hospital trips and subsequent lying down. I am told
that the ambience of London did indeed change, and that
there was a general mood of happiness and excitement
throughout July and August 2012, but I had other things
on my mind at that point. I do recall Danny Boyle's highly
sentimental but politically charged opening ceremony,
with its celebrations of the NHS and other welfare-
state institutions, in the context of the Tory/Lib Dem
coalition government that was determined to starve
them in the name of private rescue later down the line.
I also remember seeing Usain Bolt on a television screen
at some point, but otherwise the Olympics slipped past
me, and I remember nothing of the crowds or the festival
atmosphere.

After the Olympics, everything was closed again
for the physical conversion of the park from "Games
mode" to "Legacy mode", with hoardings up around
the perimeter again. If you hadn't visited the Olympics
during the Games you would still only know the
landscape from television and the windows of trains,

and it would be nearly two years before the park and the Orbit reopened in April 2014. Once it was open, however, the cracks in the Orbit's case for existence appeared very quickly.

In the original business plan for the tower the estimate of the number of visitors per year was put at 350,000, but in the first year of its operation it only attracted 124,000. This disappointing state of affairs, with the Orbit apparently losing nearly £500,000 in its first year, already adding nearly twenty percent to its original cost to the public of £3.1 million, meant that its operating company had to revise its predictions for visitor numbers down to 150,000.[11] Alongside, the search for alternative ways of making the Orbit pay had to be undertaken in earnest. More activities were planned, including abseiling down from the viewing platform, but the whole thing was already beginning to look a little bit

The Orbit - Unintended formal resonances occurred even within the park itself. (Image author's own).

like a public laughing stock, beyond those of us already horrified by the vacuity of its design.

One of the most common visual references given for the Orbit from the beginning was that it resembled a vast helter-skelter, and in fact, once the park reopened it was possible to pass by a children's play area whose equipment included precisely that, and it was at least mildly amusing to take an image of the two objects within the same visual frame. But then, in early 2016, it became clear that something more was to happen to the Orbit as an attempt to turn it around, when it was revealed that there actually would be a slide built into it after all, which punters could whizz down for the sum of £5, after having spent £12 getting up to the top in the first place.

The impetus for this new addition again came from Johnson, of course, who seems to have been throwing his weight around, looking for anything that would turn around the bad news regarding his mangled baby. Kapoor seems to have been put under pressure to alter the structure, and approached Carsten Höller, purveyor of art-slides, to adorn the Orbit with one of his works. It's a remarkable thing to have happened, that one art giant would be forced to graft the work of another onto their own, all for the sake of turning a profit, but it's clear yet again that Johnson was in no mood to think through what he was doing. Throwing out one of his typical mock-knowledgeable quips, he described the new arrangement as being "like Bernini adorning the work of Michelangelo",[12] which didn't exactly show any level of understanding of what an artwork may or may not be in the end.

However, it's perhaps perfect that Höller, whose varied work is overshadowed by the series of slides that he has constructed over the years for the Tate Modern, Hayward Gallery, Vitra, and many others, would provide that. He is perennially associated with "relational aesthetics", suggesting art that produces — at its best — moments of altered mental and social awareness sometimes called "micro-utopias", and at other times little more than some nice sensory spectacle to be enjoyed while lying on a beanbag. A giant slide dropping down nearly one hundred metres, agreed upon as part of a desperate money-saving exercise, is both an altogether alien experience capable of disrupting normal modes of experience, and also a desperate attempt to recover something valuable out of an object that should never have occurred were it not for the directionless energy of its commissioner.

Crossing the threshold, the entrance pavilion of the Orbit is filled with images and sketches of the raw genius that went into the design, alongside disembodied nonsenses quoted from each of the main protagonists. Paying and passing through the enclosure, one must move underneath Kapoor's giant steel bell, a discombobulating experience somewhat spoiled by the way the sensory gloom directs your attention to the evident cheapness of the tarmac surface underfoot. Lumps of the red structure set in concrete foundations are visible through the gaps to the side, but the visitor must walk towards two nondescript lift doors set into a little building at the very base of the structure, a surreal and probably unintended touch considering the knowledge of metallic chaos directly above.

The lifts are basic, without the glamour of the glass facades that many a commercial office tower now provides.

They have small porthole windows in their flank that draw attention more to the conventional steel structure that holds the lift shaft itself than to the unfolding views outside. Once reaching the top, however, the lift disgorges the visitor into the viewing platform, which feels much like a corporate office lobby before they've bothered putting the reception desk and high-back chairs in. In a nervous touch, almost as though there was an awareness of the inadequacy of the view, there are two more Kapoor artworks embedded into the viewing platform, concave mirrors which isolate the viewer's reflection while blurring their surroundings to the point of disorientation.

The views from the platform are fine, but lacking. One can see the City of London and Canary Wharf, but only from beneath. In fact, one can even look upwards into the upper floors of some of the neighbouring blocks of apartments that have been built across Stratford in recent years, an absurd situation for something selling itself on the view — why not just sneak into the lift at one of the neighbours? Otherwise, the stadium can be looked down into, but not from high enough to see the pitch, while the stitched-up post-industrial quality of the surrounding neighbourhoods is more than apparent. Immediately beneath, large patches of undecorated grass in the park show where new housing neighbourhoods are to be built, as over the years the "Olympic Fringes" are developed. The platform itself sits within a spread ring of the structure, and from close up one can see all the extra bracings and strange clashes of the structure that the computers deemed necessary to have it all stand up.

The disappointment of the views to the exterior are at least partly enlivened by the views to the interior. The platform has been built with a pocket in the centre, a hole that runs vertically through, like a courtyard with a ninety-metre drop beneath it. On the one hand, it makes the embarrassing cheapness of the platform all too apparent, but it also offers views directly down, and through the structure, which is perhaps the most interesting of all the views, including as it does the regular stream of punters throwing themselves down the slide. Looking down into the narrow glass-topped tunnel, able to see the drop directly beneath it, is a fragile and slightly unnerving sight, and not an experience I was particularly inclined to involve myself in, watching the vibrations of the tensile rods holding the tube in its precarious position.

Returning to ground level from the platform one can walk gradually down a spiral staircase, with perforated steel floor, walls, and ceiling. The need for structural integrity and barriers against escaping mean that the views are difficult to focus upon, making what ought to be the most interesting part of the experience — passing around and through the different spatial conditions created by the structure — more of a blurry chore, one that isn't exactly helped by a series of found-sound recordings of local environments, a nice enough idea somewhat ruined by being broadcast on tinny little speakers that render the sounds indistinguishable. Eventually the coil of the staircase unwinds and one passes through a turnstile to exit the Orbit, with only a very forlorn-looking gift shop left to experience.

Admittedly, looking at the Orbit now, nearly five years old and with a growing number of excrescences sprouting across it, it's harder to be quite so offended as I felt when it first appeared as an impossibly glossy render supplied to

Kapoor and Höller - The farce of adding fairground attractions to the structure begins to enrich the mess of it all. (Image author's own).

the press. At that point I felt almost personally attacked, as an example of some of the laziest thinking in art and architecture got firmly pressed onto the public, at a time when we were "all in it together" and there was no money for anything. It's certainly not the case that I've warmed to it — a question-begging but recurring argument for the Orbit's qualities in the early days was the fact that the Eiffel Tower was near-universally hated at first, and there's little hope for this unconvincing scramble of ideas ever becoming something truly loveable. But looking up from beneath, the more cluttered and flawed it becomes, and the more its foolishness becomes apparent, the less it seems like a victory of idiocy and more like a momentary hysteria that many involved would rather they could get away from, except perhaps the one person who actually could walk away with the greatest ease.

"Earth hath not anything to show more fair"

The Emirates Air Line

Long before the Lea Valley's transformation into the Olympic Park, another Thames-side industrial zone was reinvented as a landscape of leisure and entertainment, with similarly ambiguous results. The Greenwich Peninsula was once an area of heavy industry, being home to the Greenwich Gas Works, a vast factory complex that, upon its closure in 1985, left the entire area deeply contaminated. This charred and toxic isthmus was chosen to be the home of the Millennium Experience, the white elephant that was the source of much mirth directed at the New Labour government before the mood changed after the September 11th attacks in 2001.

Blair's government had taken the already extant proposals for a celebration of the millennium and vastly inflated them, with the oft-told story recounting that Peter Mandelson was looking to emulate the success of his grandfather Herbert Morrison's contributions to the Festival of Britain in 1951. The comparisons were vivid, both featuring social-democratic governments putting on pageants of progress and encouragement. But where the Festival of Britain was a gift for a still war-ravaged country and an initiation into the atomic age, the Millennium Experience was a celebration of the year 2000 for a country that was experiencing the short euphoria of having shaken off eighteen years of Thatcherite government. If there was an initiation at work, it was perhaps to do with the age of the internet and the digital economy, a far harder vision to sell in the era of home computers and dial-up modems.

The centrepiece of the celebrations was the erection of the Millennium Dome and the installation of the Millennium Experience within. The dome itself, and the design of its interior exhibitions, involved a who's-who of the British architecture scene in the late 1990s. The dome of course, with its whimsical symbolism of twelve masts, 52-metre height, and 365-metre diameter, was designed by Richard Rogers, a vastly inflated echo of his pumping station immediately across the river from a decade before. Inside, Zaha Hadid created one of her largest built works at that point with the Mind Zone, while Nigel Coates, at one stage considered to be *the* New Labour architect, despite his small oeuvre, was praised for the inhabited giants of the Body Zone. Famously, the visitor numbers across the year of the exhibition were way lower than expected,[13] an embarrassment compounded by the massive overspend in construction, although the financial impact was mostly borne by the National Lottery rather than directly from tax revenue.

The dome was an early example of Blairite regeneration, with the intention that the massive investment on that one particular project would then bring in the developers. Terry Farrell produced a masterplan in 1999, dividing the peninsula into a variety of different plots for individual housing developments. In preparation for this, the surrounding area was almost completely remade as part of the millennium works. A single gigantic Victorian gasometer still survives from the old gasworks, but otherwise the landscape was completely flattened, apart from the Blackwall Tunnel approach road that continues to thunder its way slowly beneath the river to the west, and to the east a short row of quaint terraced houses that were the location for the video to Blur's song "Parklife".

As part of the Jubilee Line extension, one of the most impressive examples of public works in the UK since the Thatcher era, a new station of North Greenwich was designed by Will Alsop, and further south, the Millennium Village was built to fairly generic designs that were descended at some remove from original proposals by Ralph Erskine, the architect of the celebrated Byker Wall estate in Newcastle. Before construction this housing estate was anticipated as an exemplary model for the future development of London, but the execution was underwhelming and left much to be desired, which in the end was basically accurate.

The relative flop of the Millennium Experience led to years of uncertainty for the dome, but eventually it was rebuilt within and reopened in 2005 as the O2, a large concert hall situated in its centre, and surrounding it a mock-street of deliciously fake buildings within buildings, like a polystyrene Miami trapped under a sky that is always the dreariest of greys. After a few early visits to the O2 it occasionally felt like the worst kind of space, an airport without the promise of travel, a mall with nothing much to buy, but it has become a successful part of London nightlife, both for large events, such as Vegas-style concert residencies from the likes of Bon

Jovi, but also on a normal weekend where its bars and clubs are popular, if not exactly fashionable.

Many years have passed, but the Greenwich Peninsula remains largely empty and underdeveloped. The Millennium Village is still isolated, turning its back on the carnage to the north and facing itself back towards its "ecological park". Much of the rest remains either wasteland or surface car parks, awaiting development that has, despite London's insane property market, been almost a generation in coming, although there are one or two sites that already have their generic residential towers ready. The original Farrell masterplan is still generally intact, although the site has been sold and resold a number of times, currently owned by a Hong Kong developer called "Knight Dragon", who have at least accelerated the process of development, whilst controversially reducing the amount of affordable housing. Recently, superstar architect-engineer Santiago Calatrava was announced as the designer of a £1 billion development near the dome, although if his recent projects are anything to go by it'll be a long time coming.

Immediately south of the dome, Foreign Office Architects, who provided the original radical masterplan for the Olympic Park, built one of their only major British buildings when they created a new campus for the Ravensbourne College of Design and Communication, which opened in September 2010. It's an odd building, with a skin made of tessellated tiles with a fractal geometry, occasionally punctuated by portal windows. The college has an ethos of vocational and industrially linked training, and the architects claimed that the new

The O2 landscape - Ravensbourne College sits within an incredible neoliberal landscape, almost thrillingly placeless and un-civic. (Image author's own).

buildings exemplified this more consumer-focussed form of education, a deliberate staking of ground in the new educational landscape of high tuition fees and obsessive ranking of information.[14]

Ravensbourne partially completes the strange landscape around the dome, which could at a stretch be described as a "public space" of some kind. The route that passes from North Greenwich Station to the dome has a canopy, but surrounding it are all manner of pavilions and hoardings, a free-for-all of property advertising and opportunistic commerce, all dropped down onto a sea of barely differentiated tarmac. Indeed, since 2012, an extra tensile structure has run directly across the dome of the O2, an additional attraction whereby visitors can — for a not-insubstantial fee — climb right across the roof of the dome. This testifies to the Klondike quality of much of

London, whereby no available surface, no potential view, no possible opportunity for some kind of commercial "experience" is left unexploited. If you were looking for a picture of a totally un-civic public landscape, with no representative function other than to indicate the potential of purchase, then here is an excellent example.

To the immediate south of Ravensbourne are two office blocks designed in a slightly-more-than-generic format by Terry Farrell and partners, which clearly derive much of their appearance from the building next-door, while the frames of two buildings are — at the end of 2016 — rising up behind them. Until recently, the area to the immediate south was covered in two massive inflatable sheds, which once held the David Beckham Football Academy, but these lightweight echoes of industrial sheds have been relocated, and the

Emirates Greenwich Peninsula - Is it a tube station? Is it a fairground ride? Is it a PR gimmick? (Image author's own).

site is now another car park. But tucked in behind these buildings, facing obliquely off to the water, there is a cable-car station.

A cable-car station? What on earth is this? There are no ski slopes nearby, that's for sure. A trip across the river can be achieved by going underground and taking one stop along the Jubilee Line, so what is going on? From the riverbank small boxy cars are spat forth roughly every thirty seconds, and are carried up and across the Thames by a series of three giant steel pylons, diminishing off into the middle distance. Approaching from this direction the pylons take their place amongst the cigar-shaped pylons of the dome (themselves reminiscent of the much-missed "Skylon" sculpture from the Festival of Britain), and of course the steel cranes whose strainings are gradually filling up the wasteland of the peninsula.

The station itself is a glass-clad oval structure, and is called "Emirates Greenwich Peninsula". To approach it is to be struck by the coexistence of two separate identities at once. The famous London transport roundel is highly visible, signifying that this is part of the public-transport network of the city, but it is accompanied by the typeface and colours of Emirates, the national airline of the UAE. Moving through, this confusion becomes even stronger. If this is a transport hub, why does it have the queuing fences associated with a funfair? If it's an attraction, why does it have the same ticket barriers as the tube network? But if it's a part of the public-transport network, why are the tickets referred to as "boarding passes", and why do the staff wear a uniform based upon that of a cabin crew? Why is there muzak playing in the station as people arrive to board the cars? Why is there a banner that says

"See London as you've never seen it before"? Why do the staircases encourage visitors to "Share the view from your journey #MyEmiratesView"? Why is there a gigantic jet engine just lying around outside?

One passes through the tube's electronic gates, but then must join a supervised queue to get into the gondolas. Once on board, all the questions about the split identity fade: as the car trundles upwards, it is purely experience. Beneath, on a jetty, a large steel sculpture by Antony Gormley, depicting a nude human figure, presumably his, comes into view, and one can stare into the distance and see the coils of the Orbit, and think of the opportunity Gormley missed, or perhaps the bullet that he dodged. And as the car lifts up to its highest point, the sheer mess of London in this area becomes clear. Much like with the Orbit, the actual

The view from the cable car - post-industrial, post-Blairite, uninspiring. (Image author's own).

views from this point include areas like Canary Wharf, but viewed from beneath, while the more immediate surroundings tend to be awkward juxtapositions of transport infrastructure, industrial waterside space, and the various different attempts made over the years to convert this area to residential use. Time may well change this evaluation, but at the current point the landscape as seen is one of dilapidation, of low density, little life, and, from the heights above the grey-green Thames, perhaps a little melancholy.

The slow pace of the trip, bobbing in the winds above the water, also puts paid to the idea that this is a functional, useful part of the transport network. This is a mobile twitching post, from which the gradual process of post-industrial regeneration can be viewed for as long as it might take. After a few minutes of "flight" (as the branding calls it), conducted in what should be breezy silence but is actually droned over by various nuggets of history and promotional opportunities (including, apparently, champagne evenings going round and round on the cable car), the ride begins to descend again, as it passes the third of the giant steel pylons, whose elegant twisting forms, easily the most interesting part of the project, were designed by Wilkinson Eyre. In fact, these are not the only contribution to the area from these stalwarts of the UK architecture scene, for as the car descends it comes down to another docking station, this one jutting out at an angle into the Royal Victoria Docks. This lets you off immediately across from the Crystal, whose odd folds and angles — themselves designed by Wilkinson Eyre — can be perused from above as the journey comes to an end amongst the lost apartments of the dockside.

#

The cable car was yet another project that was announced without warning, in early July 2010. A Transport for London press release with quotes from Johnson announced that it would be "a unique and pioneering addition to London's skyline" (among many, one might think) "but also offer a serene and joyful journey across the river." People would be able to "drink in the truly spectacular views of the Olympic Park and iconic London landmarks", presumably as those in the viewing platforms of the Orbit looked back and enjoyed the views of the new cable car.[15]

Coming as it did only a couple of months after the government had swapped to the Tory/Lib Dem coalition, and as the Orbit was getting ready to rise from the ground, it felt a little like another slap in the face. What was it for? Who was going to pay for it? What was the point? Why even bother? It is the case that there has been a long-running question about the state of the river crossings of London, with demand for upgraded access across the river a perennial question in the east, seeing as between the nearby Blackwall Tunnel and the Dartford Bridge there is a twenty-kilometre gap where the only vehicle crossing is either a ferry or a pedestrian tunnel. The cable car was offered as a potential solution to this issue, but in all the wrong ways — not a useful location, not a high-capacity form of transport, simply not worth it.

The cable car was also tied into the question of the Olympics — the O2 and the Excel Centre across the river were both venues for events, so the cable car was said to be servicing the demand for travel between them. From the outset, however, the project was described as being privately funded, with a sponsor or other private-sector form of finance being sought. In this way, unlike other of Johnson's projects, the cable car didn't require a fortuitous meeting to get off the ground, but in some ways this was almost more insidious. At least Johnson announced the Orbit when he was already in possession of a guarantee of money and steel, but the nature of infrastructural construction means that it's difficult to get early commitment to something that may go over budget and over schedule.

In this case, controversy was not long in coming. The budget for the cable car rapidly grew from an initial estimate of around £20 million to over £60 million, and there were fears that the structure would not be ready in time for the Olympics. The project was in a state of uncertainty for over a year, and evidence has emerged from the Leveson Inquiry in the aftermath of the phone-hacking scandal that showed that Johnson was in discussions with News International with a view to getting them to sponsor the cable-car scheme. The specific problem that emerged from this is that Johnson made loud public statements about how the phone-hacking scandal was entirely made up by disgruntled Labour politicians, right at the point when he was attempting to secure the sponsorship. A cynical mind might conclude that he was open to being bought. Whatever the motivation, the NI offer fell through.[16]

Then, in early October 2011, TfL finally announced that a sponsor had been found, and Emirates would be sponsoring the cable car. The connections to be made are quite obvious, and a fair amount of generally vacuous PR work has gone into the process — the costumes, the air-travel metaphors — so it's abundantly clear what Emirates might find attractive. Again, the prospect of being on show during the Olympics must have been very appealing to their marketing department. But from the off, there were issues. The sponsorship deal was worth £36 million, over the course of ten years. This would have nicely covered the build cost if it had been kept to the original estimate, but again the public — in the form of TfL — were forced to make up the difference.

The second issue was that the sponsorship deal encroached heavily into the territory of public transport. The inclusion of the cable car as part of the iconic London Tube map meant that for the first time the name of a commercial entity made its way onto the map. This may not seem particularly troubling, especially when the thing in question is a novelty after all, but there is concern that this opens up the gates for other such deals. In recent years the Tube map's legendary clarity has suffered greatly from the inclusion of many routes that used not to be on there, but it does seem like yet another part of the capital that is casually put up for sale.

However, the problems didn't end there. Emirates may be a luxury airline with an excellent reputation, but it is a state-run company of the United Arab Emirates, the not-uncontroversial absolute monarchy in the Gulf. Oil- and gas-rich but famously keen to diversify into finance, tourism, and culture, they have been attempting to set up a living for themselves when the oil either runs out or can no longer be burned. The UAE, especially

Dubai, are the pioneers of the 21st-century architectural spectacle, home to the tallest building in the world, the most luxurious hotel in the world, the largest mall in the world, not to mention their infrastructural efforts at building decorative landscapes right out into the sea. The phrase "Dubai on Thames", coined by Johnson himself of course, has been bandied about over the years to describe the dubiously enthusiastic constructions of the property boom, but it is more true in the sense that the Emirati have shown what can be achieved in the field of architecture as experience and spectacular attraction, an ethos that has clearly influenced Johnson.

The Emirati are also known for their dangerous and exploitative labour practices, especially in construction, with repeated accusations of the use of slave labour, as well as their draconian penal system that has been seen to imprison women for extramarital sex after they reported being raped, to give just one example. But when controversy did come to the cable car, it was in the form of old-fashioned Middle Eastern politics: a year into the deal it was uncovered that the contract for the sponsorship included a clause that prohibited TfL from making any deals on the cable car, selling a part, or putting it up as security, to:

> any person who is a national of, or who is registered, incorporated, established or whose principal place of business is in a country with which the United Arab Emirates does not at the date of this Contract or at any relevant point during the Term maintain diplomatic relations.[17]

Despite this apparently being a fairly standard clause within such contracts, it was pointed out that this deal would forbid TfL doing business with any Israelis, seeing as the UAE does not recognise Israel or maintain any diplomatic ties with them.

The clause was quickly amended, but the incident showed up yet again the lack of attention that Johnson would give to issues under his control. It was egg on his face, but it was interesting that another politician, say, Livingstone, would never have been given the benefit of the doubt on a mistake such as this.

\#

The cable car was, in the end, opened in time for the Olympics. But it wasn't very long afterwards that the warnings that were made beforehand began to come true. The cable car, quickly nicknamed "The Dangleway", was failing to perform. Like the Orbit, there were enthusiastic numbers estimated for visitor figures, but it was clear very early on that the car wasn't going to live up to the initial hype. The Olympics saw the amount of journeys reaching close to 200,000 a week, but within a year afterwards the trip numbers were all the way down to an average of about 20,000 a week, numbers that are far from enough to ensure the profitability of the service. It also later became apparent that, contrary to all the assertions early on in the process, there were only four people actually using the cable car as a commute to and from work.

This all raises the question of what the cable car actually is. If it was simply a tourist attraction, then the problems would not be particularly relevant, as long as whichever company ran it wasn't allowed to dip its fingers in the public purse to make up its losses. But its consideration as part of the transport network meant that the cable car was able to access funds that it would otherwise have to raise itself, eating into the budget for an already cash-strapped TfL. This casual disregard for the boundaries of public and private is quintessentially Johnsonian, something that followed him throughout his tenure, making luridly apparent one of the prime criticisms of the neoliberal _weltanschauung_ — a vocal contempt for the state but a consistent eagerness to use it as a source of funds and protection.

A comparison here is apt. As well as the Millennium Dome, another significant late-1990s entertainment project in London was the London Eye. Originally called the Millennium Wheel, this is a huge Ferris wheel on the Thames, situated just outside County Hall, where the GLC were once based, now home to attractions like an aquarium and the London Dungeon. Elsewhere, there had once been a giant wheel at Earls Court, built in 1895 and demolished ten years later, which like many a London attraction provided a precedent tinged with nostalgia for the later attempt.

This new wheel was the brainchild of architects Julia Marks and David Barfield, and was paid for privately by British Airways, who were its primary sponsors for the first few years of its existence. At 135 metres tall it was for a few years the tallest in the world, a useful selling point, and it has been a remarkable success, with millions of paying visitors, genuinely becoming a part of the public and world image of London. A sign of its acceptance and success is that it very rarely generates any kind of headlines, except perhaps in 2015 when its branding was taken over by Coca-Cola, on which news health campaigners heaped opprobrium.[18]

The London Eye provides the model for many of Johnson's pet projects, in particular the cable car, for which the parallels — a short vertical ride, the involvement of an airline — are clear. But the success of the Eye is clearly not easily replicated, sitting as it does in a perfect London tourist location, and with its generally clean financing. It's clearly not a particularly sensible or original course of action to just sling up as many elevated viewing experiences as possible, whilst rinsing the public purse for whatever you can grab, all the while negotiating inadequate sponsorship deals that give away far too much.

It is a shame, because the cable-car project began with a goodwill that it perhaps did not deserve. In recent years, cable cars have become known as a highly innovative solution for some of the worst urban ills. Most famously in Medellin, Columbia, or Caracas, Venezuela, but in other locations since, informal settlements have been tied back into the cities that economically depend upon them whilst simultaneously politically banishing them. By clearing only small amounts of land for the stations and the pylons, neighbourhoods where it would once take hours on foot on extremely steep terrain to travel into the city are now directly linked on routes that take only a matter of minutes.

There are controversies with urban cable cars, especially the extent to which by connecting informal settlements they then accelerate forces of gentrification and land-value increase that threaten the lives of the residents yet further, but they are a comparatively inexpensive form of transport that has been seen to make incredible difference to cities in the developing world, and as such, their attraction as a kind of urban accessory is fairly clear.

A cable car could perhaps conceivably have been an answer to a transport question in London, perhaps further to the east where there are areas that are cut off and lacking in connections, but the problem is that the real demand is for vehicle crossings in these cases, a completely different kind of infrastructure. By yet again offering the wrong solution to a problem that didn't even really exist, the cable car has blocked off other more useful options for transport that people might actually need.

"It is the latest, greatest masterpiece of British engineering and design"

The New Bus for London

For two years, from 2014 to 2016, one of my jobs was as an architect on a construction project in Victoria, West London. Victoria Street, which runs about a mile west from Parliament Square to the rail terminus, has spent much of the last decade as an enormous building site. By the end of the 19th century it had become an area of tall, classically styled office buildings crowding the street, with a smattering of industry such as Watney's Stag Brewery; but a combination of aerial destruction in WWII, and pressure for greater amounts of new kinds of office space, meant that it was comprehensively rebuilt in the years following the war.

By the turn of the millennium, many of these post-war office buildings had become grimy and tired, their facades and mechanical systems were worn out, and their architectural form of long thin slabs set back from the street had become outmoded in an era of highly serviced open-plan office space. Unlike with housing and its concepts of inheritance and perpetuity, the economic character of rented office space means that these buildings are often built for a shorter lifespan, with the view that demolition and reconstruction is a better way of maximising returns on land values over the long term.

Under the ownership of only a few landlords, in particular Land Securities, one of the UK's main property giants, a new phase of rebuilding began, with large buildings and in some cases entire city blocks demolished, to be rebuilt in the contemporary high-specification mode: all glass, acute-but-not-too-awkward angles, pressed to the very edge of the site boundary, ready to be stuffed to the gills with the finance workers who have been spreading out from the City, the ground floors given over to all the chain sandwich bars that dominate street retail in the UK. In amongst the new office buildings are new blocks of luxury housing (including a proposed but now unlikely conversion of a 1950s tower block, to be designed by David Chipperfield, which had a rumoured budget of well over £1 billion), apparently bringing some kind of life back into an area that had a tendency to become a ghost town after the offices closed.

During this time I had to regularly travel to site meetings and inspections from the office in which I was working, which was situated in a converted Victorian school building in Clerkenwell. For well over a decade this area, just to the north of the City of London, in the vicinity of the giant Mount Pleasant mail centre, had been the main focus of the architecture and design industries. At ground level it can often seem to consist entirely of shops selling modern furniture, and above, the variety of cast-off 19th-century warehouse, office, and school buildings are home to a great number of architecture studios.

Travelling across the city to site often required a trip on the 38 bus. The 38 runs at a surprisingly high frequency — every few minutes during the day, with the chaotic effects of London traffic meaning that they are frequently to be found bunched up three in a row, a vindication of the colloquial wisdom that was supposed to have long since been forgotten in the era of frequency displays and satellite tracking. The bus approaches along Rosebery Avenue, past the Spa Green Estate, which was designed by Berthold Lubetkin and Tecton, a collection of snaking tile-clad housing blocks that heralded the UK's post-war ambitions to create new housing of high quality and resolutely modern design.

Rosebery Avenue in summer is a lush tunnel of mature trees, the extent of its canopy carved out by

The New Bus For London - Oversized, cuddly, bug-eyed. (image Creative Commons https:// commons. wikimedia.org/ wiki/File:Arriva_ London_bus_LT2_ (LT61_BHT)_2011_ New_Bus_for_ London,_Victoria_ bus_station,_ route_38,_27_ February_2012_ (2)_uncropped.jpg).

collisions with the upper corners of the buses running underneath. The 38, visible for minutes from a distance as it trundles along towards the bus stop, has quite the anthropomorphic face, with clusters of headlights set in stainless-steel plates resembling bulging, startled eyes, and its nose and mouth played by the Transport for London badge and number plates. With the combination of this chubby face and a swooping black stripe running asymmetrically across its traditionally red front, the bus looks a little bit like an upset teenage "emo" boy or, hang on, now you mention it, the furious face of a mid-rant Adolf Hitler.

Step on board the 38 bus on one of the warmer days of the summer of 2015, and the first thing that would have struck you after tapping your Oyster Card on the scanner would have been an unbearable, stifling heat. The air-conditioning systems were either negligible or malfunctioning, and the buses had no openable windows in their sleek, rounded skins, so that even when almost empty the temperature inside was prone to climbing near forty degrees. If you were unlucky to get on when it was full then the heat, dampness, and general miasma from the proximity of so many other hot and damp people was enough to drive you to despair.

The ghastliness of the sauna conditions on board this particular bus earned it the nickname of the "Roast-master", a pun on its title of the "New Routemaster", after the earlier buses that its introduction was supposed to harken back to. Its original name was the "New Bus for London", although before the overheating incidents it had been colloquially christened as the "Boris Bus". It is a unique design of contemporary bus, manufactured by

Wrightbus with design by Thomas Heatherwick Studio. It was the result of a design competition necessitated by promises made by Boris Johnson during the 2008 mayoral campaign, and remains a limited edition, found only in London, with its production run soon to come to an end with no new orders.

Underneath the skin, the Roastmaster is a strange bus, larger and heavier than the basic double-decker stock common in London and other cities. This added weight comes from the fact that it has two staircases and three sets of opening doors — in effect, it is an ordinary bus extended by an extra staircase and door at the rear. But aside from this structural extension, it has a formal and aesthetic character aside from ordinary bus stock, whose designs over the years have tended towards a utilitarian

Inside the New Bus for London - A cut above normal bus design, but let down by functional waste. (image Creative Commons https://commons.wikimedia.org/wiki/File:Arriva_London_LT7_ LT12_GHT_interior_2.jpg).

drudgery, with pastel-coloured handle structures and hard-wearing artificial materials providing efficient but hardly uplifting conditions of carriage.

Once inside the Roastmaster, however, one encounters a level of aesthetic co-ordination uncommon in transport. Recurring motifs of filleted and rounded corners are found everywhere, from the softened edges of the exterior form, to the grooves in the entrance matting; from the curving stair-edges to the moulded plastic forms that sheathe most of the actual structure of the bus. The colour scheme is based around a rich burgundy colour set off against a muted grey, with metallic elements coated a deep golden colour. Even the moquette seat coverings, so often a riotously loud smattering of colours and shapes (all the better to hide the wear of thousands upon thousands of backs and bottoms) are uncommonly muted and tasteful. On the whole, the design of the bus appears to have had a remarkable level of thought put into it, designers working towards an interior environment rather than just one of optimal clarity. The general mood aimed for seems to be that of a kind of luxuriousness, but it's a difficult character to convey when the materials themselves are the same old hard-wearing plastics.

Despite the greater attention to detail, the novelty of the new design is quickly undermined. The windows of the bus, besides being unopenable, feel remarkably small, victims of the rounded roof-line that is also the cause of many a bumped head. In some locations, such as at the back, where passengers often linger to check what's following when they wish to change bus, there is a window snaking round along the line of the additional staircase. This glazing, folded awkwardly in an attempt to get a doubly-curved mass-manufactured pane of glass, is of no use to those not actually descending the stairs. Elsewhere at the back, the extra doorway folds into the footwell in quite a dangerous fashion, and the whole ensemble is undermined by two separate bars of steel cross-bracing — clearly afterthoughts — breaking awkwardly into the carefully calibrated interior environment.

Underneath the skin, the hybrid electric/diesel engines for the buses have been prone to regular breakdowns, and due to the additional weight of the new buses, the environmental performance has actually been worse compared to other more conventional buses, soon to be rendered obsolete by the adoption of hydrogen and other new technologies. The overall impression is that of this bus being an elaborate solution to a problem that doesn't really exist, a design full of anomalies that barely improve and often hinder the experience of travelling within.

#

The problem that the New Bus for London was originally intended to solve was a classic example of Johnson's fatuous cunning. During his mayoral terms, Ken Livingstone, as part of his general project to improve the bus network, had overseen the growth of a fleet of single-deck articulated buses, as are common in continental Europe. These buses served high-frequency routes such as the 38, and were notable for the relative paucity of internal seating — they are very much rush-hour buses, intended to accommodate large numbers of standing commuters at times of peak demand. They were occasionally referred to as "the free bus", due to the fact they could be entered at multiple points along their length, thus avoiding the attention of the driver, and giving the opportunity to avoid "tapping in" with the Oyster Card. But the name that they were most regularly known by was the "Bendy Bus".

The Bendy Buses were not particularly popular vehicles. I recall being frustrated by the awkward seating arrangements, which made longer journeys less pleasant, often facing either into the centre of the bus or backwards along its length. Over the years there were also a number of accidents between cyclists and left-turning vehicles, as well as pedestrian collisions. But most of all, motorists hated them for so prominently taking up room on the roads. It wasn't enough that they were clearly more efficient at carrying large numbers than a standard bus (the necessary ultra-regularity of their lower-capacity replacements testify to that), it was their mere presence, half-way to being a communist tram, perhaps, that rubbed drivers up the wrong way.

Johnson took this resentment and ran with it. In 2007, before he was even selected as the Tory candidate, he promised that "on day one, act one, scene one", he would hold a competition to design a replacement Routemaster, those iconic red buses that feature on so many postcards and films of London, and which Livingstone had phased out of normal service completely around the same time that the Bendy Buses were brought in. Johnson was picking up on a report that had been published by the right-wing think tank Policy Exchange in 2005, that had argued for precisely this course of action. A tactic like this not only picked up on a wave of civic annoyance, but also plugged it into the seemingly inexhaustible well of negative energy that is the English taste for nostalgia.

During the 2008 campaign Johnson's attitude was referred to as the "Zone 6 Strategy", meaning that whereas Livingstone's constituency was essentially the inner city, which traditionally included those on low incomes, ethnic minorities, and the basic Labour constituency of urban workers, Johnson was aiming to pick up his vote from those towards the periphery of London, traditionally Tory voters in the suburbs and surroundings.[19] Not only are these people generally the more affluent London dwellers, but they are also those who have the least emotional connection and commitment to the functions and benefits of urban life. If you spend much of your time outside the house in a car, you will be less comfortable and concerned with the minutiae of street life and whether or not it is working.

On policies such as the congestion charge, Johnson made his promises to the motorists and the wealthy residents of West London, rather than those more likely to use public transport. The promise to bring back the Routemaster was part of this — with no real functional justification apart from the public dislike of the Bendy Buses, Johnson tapped directly into a view of the London urban landscape that only really exists in the minds of those who don't spend much time actually there. The policy had no possibility of actually improving day-to-day life in the capital — it was to be a brand-new bespoke design of what amounted to a standard bus-type, yet it could be seen as some kind of harkening back to an indeterminately better time.

Johnson managed to take this nostalgia to an extra level, however. One of the most memorable qualities of the original Routemasters that the new bus was supposed to replace was the open platform at the rear, where the rear left corner of the bus was left without cladding or doors, a vertical steel post situated in the centre of the doorway. This allowed passengers to climb on and off quickly, not only at stops but in the middle of traffic. In promising to return this feature of London life with the new bus, Johnson also managed to score points against that favourite enemy of the conservatively minded, political correctness.

Having an open back to the bus that people can simply hop on and off from is a major risk — slips on the staircase could lead to passengers falling straight out of the bus at speed, and any mistake climbing on or off the moving bus could easily lead to an amputated limb. But to point this out, never mind taking the buses out of the stock, is, to a particular way of thinking, an example of hopelessly nanny-ish behaviour. Apparently the new Routemaster bus, by bringing back the open platform, would be one in the eye for the health and safety lobby, a welcome reintroduction of thrilling risk into daily life, a point which Johnson later likened to entrepreneurialism in typically heavy-handed style:

> It is, as far as I know, one of the few recent examples of a public policy that actually gives back, to sentient and responsible adults, the chance to take an extra risk in return for a specific reward.[20]

The manifesto pledge for the 21st-century Routemaster called for a design competition that would engage world-famous designers to develop the vehicle, rather than the effectively anonymous teams who are behind the most generic examples. The competition kicked off soon after Johnson became Mayor, with an original design study by the magazine *Autocar* acting as an idea generator, in much the same way that the Paul Fryer concept had been the initial image of what would become the Orbit. This initial competition had hundreds of entries, from established designers to anyone with a bit of Photoshop skill, and ranged from some serious proposals to rather half-baked efforts. The joint winners were a company called CAPOCO, an established bus designer whose design took specific and recognisably nostalgic details from the original Routemaster, and a partnership between Aston Martin and architects Foster and Partners.

The Fosters/Aston Martin design was modern in theme, less directly modelled on the original, and featured a number of details that would find their way into the final design, such as the extensive rounding of corners and the cartoonish bug-eyes. But later in 2009, when the proposal for the bus was taken forward beyond the concept design stage, the teams involved were completely different. The contract was awarded on a competitive tender to Wrightbus, a bus manufacturer based in Northern Ireland, which allowed Johnson to crow about the British jobs that the commission had created. But the design for the bus that was finally unveiled was that of Heatherwick Studio.

#

Thomas Heatherwick is one of the UK's great design success stories, a maverick with a disregard for ordinary disciplinary boundaries, a symbol of the talent and innovation coming out of the British creative industries, an eccentric possessed by the spirit of the great engineers and inventors. His work has represented Britain on the world stage on a number of occasions, and his commissions have gradually grown to the point where he is successful in the global market. But he has also been associated with a number of prominent failures, has been accused of plagiarism, and has been involved in some deeply controversial projects that threaten to ruin the reputation of anyone associated.

The Heatherwick myth usually begins with a story about him studying design at the RCA in the early 1990s, where it was said he simply didn't fit in, being, of course, too much of a maverick. Others who were there at the time report disdain for the hugely self-confident, ambitious young man, who eventually was taken under the wing of Terence Conran, who apparently recognised a talent that Heatherwick's tutors had failed to see, calling him "the Leonardo da Vinci of our times". Soon after graduating Heatherwick was able to set up a studio, and it wasn't long before his work had people taking notice.

Some early projects demonstrate what appeals about Heatherwick — operating on a variety of different scales, designing landscapes and buildings with the tactile and functional qualities of small objects, and vice versa. A small bridge over a canal dock in Paddington, London, built in 2002, coils up into a tight ball when the dock needs to be open, and slowly unfurls like a leaf when it is to be used. A public landscape in Newcastle, made of stones impregnated with crushed blue glass, folds up at the edges as if it were actually a fabric carpet, while a collection of workspaces in the Welsh woods appear to have been clad in crumpled tin foil. All of these early works, and other examples of products, furniture and artworks, had an immediacy and an ingeniousness that stood them apart from almost anything on an architectural scale being produced at the time in the UK.

Larger, more significant commissions were soon forthcoming. In 2005 Heatherwick built a gigantic steel sculpture for Manchester, which was intended to commemorate the 2002 Commonwealth Games. "B of the Bang" was a reference to a quote from the sprinter Linford Christie, and consisted of numerous giant steel spikes welded to a central core, that appeared almost like a photograph taken at the instant of a large explosion. It was a stunningly alien object, with a violent quality due to all the spikes, and at fifty-six metres it was at that point the tallest sculpture in the UK, all of which echoes forward to the Orbit nearly ten years later.

More success soon followed. Heatherwick's "Seed Cathedral" was the UK's pavilion at the Shanghai Expo of 2010, and featured a similar "fuzzy" form, originally developed for a small pavilion he built in 2003. Over 60,000 acrylic rods were embedded into the building, each containing a different kind of seed, representing the relationship of nature and cities, while the pavilion was laid on a landscape that was folded like crumpled paper, as if the whole thing had just been unwrapped. The pavilion was hugely successful, offering an idea of remarkable clarity, with just the right vague touch of environmentalism, which stood out clearly against the cluttered complexity of many of the other architectural efforts.

By this point Heatherwick had clearly proven himself as a brand ambassador for the UK, and another set of commissions would really drive this home — the Cauldron for the London Olympics, the New Bus for London, and later, the Garden Bridge. Heatherwick was directly commissioned by Danny Boyle for the Olympic gig, and the bright idea was that the Cauldron would be made out of a series of individual metallic "leaves" that were brought into the stadium by representatives from competing nations, affixed to long "stalks", which then at the required moment would rise up together to constitute one single flame. It was simple, ingenious, and — thankfully, considering the sheer number of moving parts — worked. As a symbol of the 2012 Olympics, of Britain's ingenuity in an era of no longer being a major world power, it couldn't have been much better.

But Heatherwick doesn't only gather rave reviews and positive headlines. There have been a string of major failures that have gone along with his career, and other controversies as well, meaning that his reputation is not quite as smoothly glowing as it appears from some directions. A major early problem was with the "blue carpet", which within a few years was suffering from decaying materials that required costly replacements. Later on, a similar backfiring innovation left major egg on his face when the B of the Bang sculpture began to break down. A small number of spikes either fell to the ground or came loose, and the resulting repair costs were enough for the council to order the removal of the sculpture to storage. Heatherwick was forced to pay damages over this incident, and was then further dragged through the mud over a question of attribution relating to the Olympics.

It seems that in the years running up to the Games, a remarkably similar concept for a canopy formed of petals, to be brought together from all the different competing countries and assembled within the stadium, had been presented to the Olympic organising committee long before Heatherwick got involved. The company in question, an American design practice called Atopia, had been involved in early conceptual design, but had been prevented from speaking out about the work they had done because of confidentiality agreements. What appears to have happened is either that Heatherwick was given a brief based on the original concept, which he was then free to develop as his own, or worse, that the early report itself was used as the basis of his design. The cauldron case would eventually be settled out of court a year later, with Atopia given acknowledgement of their work, along with a sum of money, but with Heatherwick able to deny any suggestion that he was a plagiarist.

In 2012 I interviewed Heatherwick for a short article after the studio won a prize for the Olympic Cauldron. It had been a good year for him, as the New Routemaster was going into production at that point, so hadn't had a chance to display its troubles, and there were new architectural projects on the horizon. The office was a beautifully fitted-out set of warehouses hidden down a lane from a street near Kings Cross, with large workshops alongside the design areas, and big moveable walls for separating off meeting rooms, themselves decorated by a collection of stunning relief maps. He played the role of the absent-minded genius well, pausing for long periods while he searched for phrases, and displaying a childish enthusiasm for his endeavours. He is very charming, a little bit dashing, and generally says just the right thing, seasoned interviewee that he is, although there is perhaps a naivety to his delivery that is a little bit too affected.

As far as the bus is concerned, the stylings of Heatherwick Studio can't really be said to have contributed to the problems of the batteries or the poor air-conditioning. The quest for an iconic form might have been to blame for the windows, but the majority of the buses' flaws were right there in the brief, and it would be churlish to deny that the design itself attempts to bring a little thought and consideration to what can be a joyless world of public transport. The Roastmaster was a close shave, but Heatherwick could still hold his head up at this point, his star still ascending.

#

Today in London, one can occasionally see original Routemaster buses travelling through the city, maintained as they are on a few "heritage" routes, with others still in use as private-hire vehicles for weddings and other such trips. They remain a large part of the heritage industry, with their imagined connections to "swinging" London and the 1960s, forever tied together with images of the Houses of Parliament, dome-helmeted policemen, and other vital symbols of British tourism.

Seen in today's context though, the Routemaster is a strange affair. It is notably smaller than the current generation of buses, clear from the outside but relatively uncomfortable on the interiors. But it also appears extremely light. The first reason for this is the two major cutaway sections of the bus. Whereas most contemporary stock is clearly a full box, firm right to the outside, the Routemaster has the rear opening, and at the other end the famous cut-out section above the engine. This missing area gives the entire bus a strange weightless appearance, with the upper deck cantilevered out over the shortened ends. It's a completely different feeling to that of the hulking New Bus for London.

The forward cutaway means that the driver of the Routemaster was somewhat isolated from the passengers, with windows on three sides of their seating. This cab bears more than a passing resemblance to the cockpit of a WWII fighter plane such as the Spitfire, and for good reason — the Routemaster, developed from the late 1940s, used technologies developed in the aircraft industry during the war, in particular the aluminium-bodied Halifax bomber, to make a cheap, lightweight vehicle for peacetime. The body of the bus was made from aluminium, and its folded corners and lightweight riveted appearance were — at the time — signs of advanced manufacturing in a time of austerity.

So while on the one hand the Routemaster epitomises a particularly nostalgic view of the UK, often appearing alongside some rather conservative symbols, not to mention the associations with the military; at the same time it is also a fragment of a very different view of the UK's history, that of the forward-looking, high-technology egalitarian society that at certain points in the post-war era it looked like the UK might become. For example, in Patrick Keiller's films *London* and *Robinson in Space*, the Routemaster appears as an "undeniably utopian" symbol of the lost promise of the UK, destroyed by Thatcherism and the nostalgia industry. But there isn't even a hint of that spirit in the New Bus for London.

The New Bus for London is considered — when not overheating or breaking down — to be a pleasant bus to drive, although its extra size and weight are not always appreciated. It was even quite popular with commuters, and I'd readily admit that waiting to jump off the platform at the back was at least a little bit exhilarating. But it wasn't long before even this was under threat — the conductors at the back of the bus, paid to ensure some kind of health and safety, were laid off to cut costs, leaving the back doors reduced to standard functioning. Meanwhile, other bus companies got their game together and included some Heatherwick-esque styling in their new standard models, thus including the positive aspects of the bus without carrying over the expensive frivolities.

But the argument for the New Bus for London that comes closest to justifying it, is to see it as a ready-made attraction. The bus wasn't really for the inhabitants of the city who use the bus every day, it's not even really for the sake of the Zone 5 & 6 weekenders. If it really has a purpose, it's for the millions of people who visit London every year, to create something that functions adequately for the contemporary age that also connects to the worldwide brand represented by the city. It may not have been a Routemaster that was taken to Beijing in 2008 for the closing ceremony of the Olympic Games, as a foretaste of what was to come in 2012, but this sense of the iconic nature of the big red bus was the same spirit that fed into its creation.

As far as Johnson is concerned, this just shows yet again how his conception of his responsibility as the Mayor of a world city barely stretched past the idea of effectively being a sales rep, a gimmick merchant for the tourists. In this way, the millions spent on developing and manufacturing a fleet of buses that has had no impact elsewhere, and indeed will be phased out soon enough as new low- and zero-carbon vehicles hit the road, is conceptually little more than the production of all those fridge magnets, tea towels, plastic toys, and of course pictures of Johnson, that fill the tat shops that line Shaftesbury Avenue.

But the really remarkable thing about this is again the fact that it happened — that an idea so pointless was stage-managed and greased through by the sheer gumption and gusto of the Mayor. There was no need for it, it didn't work, and there won't be any more of them, but even so, he got them built.

"A spirit of invention which was to shape London and the world for generations to come"

The ZhongRhong Crystal Palace

Sydenham is a neighbourhood of London approximately ten kilometres due south from the centre, located within the initial ring of suburban neighbourhoods surrounding the inner city proper. It thus lies just within the traditional Labour voting core of urban London, although at the same time it finds itself at the northern end of the Tory-controlled borough of Bromley. It is not quite far enough out of the centre to feel anti-urban, the sort of place from which Johnson primarily drew his support, but it lacks the sheer density of city activity that can be found further in.

Unlike the inner core of the city, however, Sydenham is hilly, with a landscape of rolls and falls that feels incongruous when you are used to the pancake-flat steppes of areas closer to the river. It is very leafy, with much of the neighbourhood given over to woods and parks, but it also feels this way in part due to the low density of buildings, with large areas taken up by detached Victorian villas, once home to well-off families, now subdivided, and the medium-density private apartment blocks that are their post-war equivalents.

This area and its neighbours, including Penge and Gypsy Hill, were largely off my radar in my first years in London, seeing as this was part of a series of neighbourhoods around Dulwich that I presumed were for people older and richer than I, a place for highly paid thirty-somethings to move to when settling down with their family, perhaps. If you do not look closely enough, there is a tendency for outer areas of London to blur together, to become just one of a series of mainly residential zones that have been absorbed by the metropolis over the years. But gradually a specific interest meant that I was drawn to visit the area repeatedly.

One of the most striking landscapes in the area, if not the whole of London, is Crystal Palace Park. This large public park, shaped something like a heraldic shield, slopes down to the east off from the Norwood Ridge, a one-time source of many of the London bricks that gave 19th-century London its particular visual and tactile quality, and that contribute much to the apparent homogeneity of the city suburbs. Within the park's two hundred acres are a variety of strange and wonderful structures, buildings, sculptures, and infrastructure, and one particularly colossal absence.

The land that makes up the park was once called Sydenham Hill, and was until the mid-19th century still in the countryside way outside of London, before the railway boom created the sprawl that so defines it now. On the site stood a country house called Penge Place, which in 1854 was purchased and demolished by the Crystal Palace Company, headed by Joseph Paxton, who were looking for a location to rebuild the iron and glass hall of the Great Exhibition of 1851. Originally intended as a temporary shed, the palace had been removed from Hyde Park a few years previously, but the success of the exhibition had raised the question of how to maintain the feelings of pride that had come from it, and subsequently the Royal Commission for the Exhibition of 1851 used the profits to establish "Albertopolis", where the V&A, the Natural History and Science Museums, Imperial College, the Royal Albert Hall, and the Royal Colleges of Art and Music are all still located.

The shed had been taken down, but then in a spirit of optimism and with funds raised by public subscription, the palace was rebuilt as an educational and entertainment facility at the top of the Sydenham Hill, with Paxton laying out the rest of the land as a series of extravagant formal gardens with ultra-powerful fountains. The park, which at first was accessible only by an entrance fee, thus making it the forerunner of latter-day amusement parks, was connected to the city by two separate brand-new railway stations, which allowed the palace to cater to the weekend recreation of the new middle classes, and also encouraged the surrounding neighbourhood to develop into a bourgeois suburb of London.

The Crystal Palace stood in the park for eighty-two years, although it did not have a smooth run of things. Paxton's overspend on the park itself meant that the company went bankrupt soon after opening, an event repeated in 1911 after which the palace and park had to be completely taken over by the state. After a period as the first permanent home of the Imperial War Museum in the 1920s, the palace became increasingly run down in the years following, although the 1930s saw some serious investment in the hope the palace could be made to work financially. Eventually, however, the palace burned down

Crystal Palace Park - A sense of melancholy emptiness, ripe for redevelopment. (Image author's own).

in a massive conflagration on 30th November 1936, after which it was cleared away, leaving the symmetrical and ornate park without its main focal point.

When I first visited on a crisp and cold afternoon one early spring, the sense of this gigantic absence was the defining characteristic of the park. The area upon which the palace stood remains mostly empty, although areas have been put to use. At one entrance to the park is a small garden, next to a plot that has been given over to an open bus terminus. However, much of the footprint is simply rough ground, with occasional inconclusive foundations poking through, while some of it is now an area of fenced-off forest.

Another patch to the north, just south of a caravan park, is also closed off as it houses the Crystal Palace Transmitter, which was the tallest structure in London from the 1950s until One Canada Square was completed in Canary Wharf in 1990. This transmitter, with its faint echoes of Eiffel but also of the lightweight structure that once stood in the park, is a South London landmark visible from all over the city. At one location, the scrubland terrace has been adorned with a 1:1 model of a single bay of the original palace, built in steel, giving a ghostly hint of the sheer scale of what once stood on the site.

Descend the hill, through a cutting that has been carved through the foundations of the palace, and the massive staircases and terraces that once led up into the building are still in some cases there, but leading to nowhere, while statues of colonial subjects and plunder continually remind you of the bloody arrogance that fed the Victorians' pomposity. The void of the space around the palace is eerie, even slightly menacing, and at my first visit I was actually reminded of the Parade Grounds at Nuremberg, a similarly vast space completely detached from the purpose to which it was once put. The sight of huge empty terraces and ceremonial staircases is a source of some of the more ominous connotations of ruination, of imperial power and demonstrations of belligerent might.

A taste for a more indulgent, personal romanticism can also be indulged in the park, as some of the remnants of the palace have been given over to genuine decay, with ivy and all the rest of it, and the sense of melancholy is pervasive, even on the brightest and sunniest days, with the scale of the terraces dwarfing the picnics and dog walks that go on there now.

Winding through the park at this point is another strange fragment, a wide and smooth road, leading nowhere, which was at one point a motor-racing circuit. This first appeared in the 1930s and was still in use right up until the early 1970s, when it was closed down on safety and public-nuisance grounds. Cars used to stream past the terraces of the palace at over one hundred miles per hour, which, in a certain strange resonance, is a use that the Nuremberg parade grounds are also put to, the semi-ruined terrace from which Hitler once spoke now the viewing stand of the Norisring.

Heading further down the slopes, along the main ceremonial axis that used to start at the vaulted apse of the palace, you pass a gigantic stone head of Joseph Paxton, looking forlornly down and away from his lost creation. The main physical counterpart to the palace in the early years were Paxton's two fountains, fed by huge water towers designed by I.K. Brunel, which were able to spray more than 150 feet into the air. These were so expensive to maintain that by the end of the 19th century they had been filled in, given over to sporting grounds where the first few FA Cup finals were held, and where the eponymous football team once played.

So even before the end of the 19th century the park had seen all kinds of alterations and functional complications, making it into a rather conflicted and confused environment, meaning in the post-war era it was not difficult for this filled-in part of the park to become home to a large modernist sporting facility. To the south of the main axis is an athletics stadium, and to the north is the National Sports Centre, designed in the mid-1950s by Leslie Martin as part of the LCC architects department.

The NSC - Structure as metaphoric content, of athleticism, of industrial labour. (Image author's own).

The NSC is an interesting counterpoint to the swimming facility as designed by Zaha Hadid for the Olympic Park in East London. It too is accessed off a walkway that feeds into the ceremonial axis of the park, creating a raised ground level, again at a scale that only makes sense in periods of heavy use, feeling oversized and empty otherwise. The NSC building itself is large and rectangular in plan, with a central circulation space that is defined by a frame of angled concrete columns, made extremely thin by pre-tensing the steel reinforcement within them. These create a V-shaped space frame from which the roof spreads out, to one side over sports courts and to the south over an Olympic-sized pool, whose dramatically sculpted diving boards mimic the structural logic of the overall building. The tense structure to the centre of the building means that the wings spread out column-free, so that the facades to the side are remarkably light.

The Aquatics Centre plays similar games with large spans, considering the scale of uninterrupted space required for sports and swimming functions, but it demonstrates the huge conceptual differences between the modernist conception of architecture and that which is practiced by the cutting edge today. The NSC is abstract, and displays its structure as a demonstration of the work and forces that are going into its standing up, and if there is a metaphorical game being played it is that of an equivalence between the highly balanced forces of the concrete structure as a kind of athleticism of inanimate material. The Aquatics Centre, on the other hand, uses a gargantuan amount of steel structure which is completely hidden away underneath its cladding, all signs of labour or work disappeared, in favour of a general resonance between function and form, a more or less direct allusion to waves, or perhaps whales.

The NSC is currently secure, if a little dilapidated, although it wasn't quite so in recent years. A decade ago, even before the financial crisis, its maintenance requirements meant that there was a serious discussion about its demolition, a possibility now hopefully held off by its becoming a listed building. But there have been long running and sometimes controversial plans to demolish the athletics stadium, which are still floating in the air to this day.

Further down the slopes of the park one finds another fantastic London curio, the geological park, nestled into a corner at the lowest point of the park. Here a number of winding paths lead through a contrived rocky landscape, occasionally peeled back to offer a demonstration of the stratified layering of the British ground, a swiftly developing scientific field at the time that the park was laid out. And then, on artificial islands in a lake, there are the famous Crystal Palace Dinosaurs, life-size mock-ups of various extinct species, rendered in concrete, stone, lead, and latterly repaired in fibreglass and resin. I remember learning about these strange Victorian curios as a child, about the fact that the naturalist Richard Owen had originally affixed what would be later ascertained as the thumb bone onto the nose of the iguanodon, the other strange assumptions regarding form and posture from the early years of the dinosaur craze, and the famous banquet held in the mould of one of the dinosaurs, immortalised in a drawing from the *Illustrated London News*.

The whole ensemble had fallen into disrepair, but have been restored and are now a Grade-I-listed monument, the strangest of all the strange objects across the park. The disparate layers of activity over the years, the different functions that all take their place in the park, and the size and relative dilapidation, are a far cry from the order and general care taken of other parks in the centre of London. But one small thing that has changed over the years is the upgrade of the East London Line, which since 2010 has made it a lot easier for central Londoners to travel directly to the park, and stitched it a little closer into the consciousness of the city as a whole. In visits subsequent to the reopening, the new presence of East London hipsters picnicking in the park was an entertaining development.

The overground trains arrive into the Crystal Palace lower-level station, the only one remaining of the two that once served the palace, which is yet again highly oversized, designed as it was to bring thousands and thousands of visitors to the palace for day trips in the late 19th century. Now it sits in a state of partial restoration, upgraded where necessary but still cracked around the edges, a partial fragment of the state of the park beyond. Indeed, there have always been question marks hanging over thë park, its lack of clarity and multiple layers of use not only making it difficult to fund works to keep it in good condition, but also making it possible for all manner of proposals to be put forward for it, some more outlandish than others. But this has almost always been a condition of limbo, that is, until Johnson thought he had finally found the answer.

#

I was idly refreshing my browser at work one summer's day in 2013, most likely trying to put off drawing a staircase detail or filling out a door schedule, when the BBC News website mentioned that something was about to happen in London. "Plans for Crystal Palace Replica" said the headline. My first book had been published just over a year before and had a number of chapters that dealt with the Crystal Palace, and its influence over modern architecture in the century and a half since it was created, so this immediately caught my interest. My initial presumption was that someone was proposing to create a replica of a small section of the building, large enough to hold events inside perhaps — there is a history of replicated fragments of iron and glass palaces, including the single corner bay currently standing in the park itself.

But the article described something very different, something much more ambitious. It seemed that Johnson was entertaining an overture from a Chinese property developer, who was looking at the possibility of rebuilding the entire palace on the site where it once stood. I was incredulous — surely it wasn't possible that something so vast, so particularly of its time, both culturally and materially, could be resurrected that simply? The palace was built from materials that are no longer used in construction, and its vast open spaces inside would in no way meet current building regulations, particularly those, of course, related to the prevention of and escape from fire. There is a low-quality 1980s building in Dallas in the US called the "Infomart" that claims to be a replica of the Crystal Palace, but is basically a concrete-framed air-conditioned block with a facade that mimics Paxton's design, and this kind of half-baked point-missed imitation is what immediately came into mind upon the first announcement.

Then, in October 2013, the inevitable press event occurred, and Johnson revealed the plans, such as they were. ZhongRhong Group, a Chinese development company based in Shanghai, were offering £500 million to create a replica of the Crystal Palace, a proposal described as being a "culture-led exhibition space" that was to include a hotel and conference facilities, studios, galleries, and other commercial units. But what was extremely telling was how little detail there was about anything. The images released at the time showed a CGI version of the palace back on its site, looking a little ghostly perhaps, but very much the same in size, form, and construction — someone had made a 3D model based upon old photographs, and quickly knocked out some images. But the release only said that the new building would be the same size and scale of the original, which basically meant an absolutely massive building — the 1854 version was almost four hundred metres long.

The whole thing stank, on any number of levels — what on earth was the building going to be? How could Johnson just give away a huge area of a public park to a private developer? Who was this developer, for that matter? But beyond these questions, this time it almost felt personal. I'd already watched in dismay as the Orbit came about and was built, an inane travesty of the rhetoric of both public art and advanced architectural design, but as someone who had conducted a great deal of research into the history of the Crystal Palace, and had written a book, articles and had given many lectures on it, this almost felt like a slap in the face, as Johnson came riding roughshod over what is an extremely difficult and conflicted historic object, one in which I had considerable personal investment.

It's not hard to understand what was going on. Crystal Palace Park was clearly in need of investment: many areas were falling apart, there were large parts that were inaccessible, including a wonderful polychromatic brick subway that once led from the upper-level station, and the whole space had an air of sadness about it. In the years previously, a great many different schemes came and went — there was the multiplex cinema that was thwarted in the 1990s, there were underdeveloped local campaigns to somehow rebuild the palace exactly as was, and then there was a ludicrous new glass blob mooted by

Wilkinson Eyre in 2003, intended as an "Iconic!" gesture to get the investment ball rolling.

In more recent times, a major landscaping scheme had been developed that included the creation of a grove of trees planted to match the structural grid of the palace, thus creating a naturalised echo of its original form, perhaps the most appropriate treatment of the space. Elsewhere there were plans to rationalise the landscaping, create a small new museum, improve the sports facilities through the construction of a new building and the filling-in of the "moat" around the NSC, among many other improvements. The major problem that people had with this scheme, submitted for planning in 2007, was that it involved building 180 market-rate houses on the area of the caravan site and along the edge of the park, the proceeds from the sale of which were then intended to cross-fund the other works to the park.

Johnson approved of this scheme early in his tenure, even though it went against his campaign promise to "protect green space from greedy developers", and supported the argument that what was needed to safeguard the park was the selling off of parts of it. There was a vociferous local campaign against the proposals, including a high-court challenge that hinged on technicalities such as bat-roosting locations, which are legally protected. But in 2012, Communities Secretary Eric Pickles approved the outline planning scheme, which was still sitting in limbo, five years after submission, when the new proposals surfaced.

The offer from ZhongRong must have seemed far better — here was a willingness to spend half a billion pounds (probably more), with no real state involvement, that would solve the problem of the park for generations to come. Time and again Johnson showed himself to be only interested in getting stuff done, no matter what it was, so this would have been for him, as they say, a no-brainer. But there was more to it than that. There are at least two histories to the Crystal Palace, and there was clearly one at the front of Johnson's mind. Just as he used the Routemaster as a symbol of reactionary nostalgia in order to make his mayoral campaign appeal to a certain English mentality, so there is a picture of the Crystal Palace that is utterly delectable for the wistfully conservative, the harkers-back to better days before.

In both its 1851 and 1854 versions, the Crystal Palace was taken to be a symbol of Britain's dominance in the world. It was a symbol of ingenuity, of industrial prowess, but also of magnanimity and culture. The Great Exhibition invited the world to London in a spirit of comradeship, while the 1854 palace was intended as an improving environment in which the different social orders could mingle. Here is an image of Victorian boldness and vaulting achievement that has time and time again been absolute catnip for the conservative mind, of buccaneering entrepreneurship, of risks and rewards won, but also of giving back, of the congruence of interests of different social classes.

But a great deal of scholarship has also been produced that shows the other side of the history of the Crystal Palace, of the fears of revolution that it was thought to be a chance to quell, of its vision of a future technologically ordered society without divisions, of its repeated financial failures and its exposure of the limits of human needs faced with the apparent limitlessness of humanity's technical abilities. None of these more nuanced or conflicted aspects of the building would have played much of a role in anyone's considerations, and the project was initially promoted largely as a chance for a great symbol of Britain's glory days to be resurrected for the 21st century.

Another design competition was organised, with a call for expressions of interest generating a shortlist of six firms, the makeup of which tells its own interesting story about the recent history of British architecture. Two of the shortlisted practices were Rogers Stirk Harbour and Partners, and Grimshaw Associates, firms most associated with the "British High-Tech" movement. This was born out of 1960s countercultural experimentalism, but gradually mutated — through years of seeking work in the politically hostile 1980s — into something that became more of a celebration of the British engineering tradition represented by Brunel or Paxton. Architects like these can present themselves as both incredibly modern but also tied to a lineage of great practical men of science, and both have made much of their debt to the engineering architecture of the Crystal Palace. With this in mind, their inclusion on the shortlist was no surprise.

Marks Barfield were on the list, which one would surmise was as a result of the success of the London Eye. They are not particularly prolific at the top level of British architecture, but that one huge success story has meant their names are still highly regarded. Another strange choice was Haworth Tompkins, who are excellent architects but generally tend to work at smaller scales and on complex briefs, frequently extensions and refurbishments of theatres, university buildings, and so on.

Two other strands of British architecture were represented by the remaining shortlisted entries. David Chipperfield has always been slightly apart from the British scene, being more aligned to intellectual currents of mainland Europe, especially Germany. His is a historically rich architecture, generally modernist but with a strong engagement with classical design, which is often compared to the luxurious quasi-modernism built in Mussolini's Italy. In recent years, however, this way of thinking about architecture has become more acceptable, perhaps due to a general conservatism in public life, and Chipperfield has become more prominent in the UK. However, it's hard to imagine two architectures less conceptually alike than Chipperfield's heavy, weighty design and the abstract shed of 1854.

The final entry on the shortlist was no surprise, but was even more telling, a potential collaboration that struck yet more fear into my heart — Zaha Hadid Architects were working with Anish Kapoor. It's only fair that ZHA had a shot in a shortlist like this, representing as they do a particular vision of "The Architecture of the Future". Against the historic continuity of someone like Chipperfield, Hadid's work was entirely in love with the new, but not necessarily in an abstract way, and as the vague formal representations that define their work (waves for a pool, dunes for buildings in the desert, etc., etc.) show, it's a spectacular futurism lacking the naked technical boldness of the Victorians. Hadid had built some large buildings in China, which perhaps could have helped with the intended global impact of the design, although it would be very unlikely that she could have designed something of her typically outlandish manner within the stated budget of £500 million.

Kapoor, however, should already have been bruised by the Orbit collaboration, and yet here he was, only two years later, putting his name forward for another dubious Johnsonian project with similarly inauspicious beginnings, especially considering the brief, or lack of it. Apparently the building was due to include an observation deck, a quintessentially Johnsonian programme, but if the building was to fit inside the original volume of the palace there wouldn't be much to see apart from Croydon. But what else? The original palace in 1854 had included two concert venues, one capable of fitting 30,000 people within it, and a series of "courts" that were replicas of periods of architectural history, filled with sculpture, art, and manufactures. It even originally included new art and design and engineering schools, and there were a wide range of tea rooms and shopping opportunities alongside. And of course, surrounding everything was the giant glass envelope that meant the entire space was treated as a winter garden, and in the early years at least it was heavily filled with greenery.

The extremely obvious yet insidious point about this situation was that the competition could be described as being for the recreation of the palace, but taken out of context, the programme suggested in the vague brief was effectively just a massive modern leisure building, not unlike the O2, with a combination of retail and leisure, and perhaps a little culture sprinkled in. But for something this big the instructions were still totally unclear, even at the point of the second stage of the competition, a problem that at the time looked terrifying, but would actually turn out to be a saving grace.

#

If Johnson was to a large extent a walking advertisement, an ambassador for the brand that is London, then there were certain contracts that were especially rich. Livingstone's famous global reach-out was securing an oil trade deal with the Chavez government of Venezuela, an entertainingly "loony-left" act of diplomacy that was reminiscent of 1980s councils renaming streets after Nelson Mandela or erecting plaques commemorating the victims of Hiroshima and Nagasaki. Johnson, upon taking office, promptly cut the deal off. For him, the only places to look for funding were among the fields of grey suits, a constituency never quite neglected by Livingstone, but definitely the pastures amongst which Johnson felt most at home.

For a number of years, China was one of the main prizes for investment, especially after the global financial crisis. This worked in an outward direction — for example, architects were just one of a number of professions that went pitching for work in the Far East, and for a number of years they were welcome, as their expertise and experience, not to mention prestige, were valued as the domestic industry was finding its feet in the global context. But while many London studios were kept afloat by designing towers and speculative projects in entirely new cities — sometimes bigger than London — in the provinces of China, there was also the question of bringing some of that new Chinese money back over.

Halfway through his tenure, it might have been said that Johnson wasn't doing all that brilliantly, with his "whiff whaff" comments at the Olympics falling somewhat flat. There was also further bad feeling in the air, after David Cameron met with the Dalai Lama in 2012, the kind of snub to the Chinese that tends to be taken seriously, and after which Beijing briefly suspended ministerial contact with the UK. So it could easily be seen as significant that the Crystal Palace rebuild project was conveniently announced only a few days before Johnson left on a trip to China to develop trade links, doing the usual thing of dodging journalists' questions regarding human rights and freedom in China, and stressing the importance of maintaining good relations with such a huge potential market. However, the Westminster government saw fit to send George Osborne to China just a day after Johnson, perhaps to keep an eye on the gaffe-prone blusterer.

Back in London, ZhongRong Group were represented by their Chairman, Ni Zhaoxing. He was a typical Chinese success story — old enough to have lived through the Cultural Revolution, taking advantage of the opportunities presented by the Deng Xiaoping era to build himself a fortune in business. The ZhongRong Group was founded by Ni and his wife — tellingly the daughter of a government administrator — through property investments beginning in the late 1990s, investing in Shanghai in the aftermath of the Asian Financial Crisis. By the time of the Crystal Palace scheme, he was said to be personally worth more than $1 billion, amongst the hundred richest people in China, with a portfolio that included not only office space and residential development (including a set of luxury villas in the Louis XIV style on the outskirts of Beijing), but also energy and infrastructure, such as shale gas investments in the US.

Within the context of Johnson's "do anything, please" attitude to development and investment, it seems that anyone offering half a billion pounds for a massive development, with the promise of potentially yet more money coming in from China in future, would of course get a quick hearing. This was especially so considering the limbo that the park upgrade works had been sat within for such a long time. But it seems there was more to this than met the eye.

Later efforts by local journalists, including freedom-of-information requests, meant that new light was shone on the process. It turned out that discussions with ZhongRong had been ongoing for as much as two years before the late 2013 announcements, and that planning advice had already been formulated regarding the potential development, sent out with a letter from the Mayor in November 2012 regarding "the exciting Crystal Palace glass-house proposal which we are keen to see progress".

The planning advice described the scheme thusly:

A recreation of the Great Exhibition glass-house buildings is proposed on the original site. Uses proposed to be contained within these buildings include a 6 star hotel, retail uses (mainly jewellery showrooms and sales) and art galleries together with 1800 car parking spaces. The floorspace proposed is 2 million sq.m.[21]

One has to wonder if the square meterage described was a mistake, considering that the massive Westfield shopping mall at the Olympics has a retail floor area literally a tenth of that size. But even beyond that, the inappropriateness of the suggested programme is astounding, making the whole thing seem as half-baked and crass as one of those brand-new luxury malls in Dubai that have mock-ancient wind towers stuck on top for a kind of "authentic" historic flavour.

The report went on to note that the proposed rebuild broke almost every planning policy on the books, in terms of scale, function, and location, noting that "by definition the development proposed is inappropriate development", but then noting that the previously approved scheme used the promise of the refurbishment of the park as an exceptional justification for building houses, so something could possibly be done on that front. Another warning can be seen in the note that as the proposed scheme was a recreation of a historic structure, "albeit taller than the original", there could be justification made. This suggests that from the very beginning the notion that this would be a "recreation" was only loosely defined at best.

The rest of the report went on to list various ways in which the development could be justified through additional works, especially refurbishments to the park as a whole, as well as transport upgrades (one of which, a Crystal Palace tram link, was part of Johnson's 2012 re-election campaign), clearly fishing for some cross-investment as a way of greasing the development gears. The final conclusion was that:

The principle of recreating the Great Exhibition glasshouses on their original site is strongly supported in terms of supporting London's World City role and achieving the exceptional strategic development of Crystal Palace as a major destination.

That might sound like positive support, but as anyone who has negotiated with the UK's planning system over the years will attest, this reads effectively as a foregone conclusion. The political will was for this project to go ahead, it was supported from the top, and thus the resistance that the planning department were already clearly anticipating would be suppressed where possible.

#

But little of this was known in 2013. The announcement may have been made in a neutral voice in the press, but quickly a basic opposition to the idea was voiced by journalists and commentators. In early 2014, after the shortlisted architects had been announced for the project, I wrote an article for the *New Statesman*, which was given the editorial title of "Boris Johnson's plan to sell public land for a new Crystal Palace will be a terrible boondoggle".[22] In the article I noted the previous Johnson vanity projects — the Orbit, the cable car, the New Bus for London, as well as the loss-making sponsorship of the cycle hire scheme. I argued that the Crystal Palace looked to be the most pointless project yet.

I noted that the brief was not for a recreation of the palace but for a new building "in the spirit" of the original, and that the brief was vague and ill-defined. The fact of the park being "Metropolitan Open Land", which legally could not be developed, the lack of demand for a building of that scale in that location, and the inability of the local infrastructure to cope, not to mention the fact that the cultural brief was so diffuse that it reeked of being cover for the construction of a shopping mall, were all outlined.

But I also noted the problems of the historic reference — the glorious symbolism of the Great Exhibition, but also the financial failures, the melancholic decline, and the utopian responses to the building. I also remarked upon the strange resonance of how the original Crystal Palace was built at a time when the British were opening China up to trade through violence, coming just before the second Opium War, and how Ni and ZhongRong Group could not possibly be unaware of this fact. What a symbol of further British decline could this turn out to be?

The article led to me being invited to speak at a local meeting regarding the developments, alongside a London Assembly member, a writer whose novel had been set in the palace, and an "enlightened" property developer who had built some high-quality housing in the local area. In a crowded hall near the top of the park I gave my short talk about the strange history of the palace and its conflicting resonances in history, which was not dissimilar to that of the author. The developer spoke about ways in which developers might work with the local community rather than against them, and the politician gave a strange speech full of disjointed-yet-rousing platitudes.

But what was remarkable about the meeting was that when all the talks were finished, and questions were opened up to the floor, each person who stood up seemed to be known to everyone else in the hall, and ignoring the invited speakers completely, proceeded to make their own short speeches themselves. It became abundantly clear that in the area there was already a strongly organised group of community activists who were already veterans of previous campaigns to protect the park (one activist spoke of people having previously chained themselves to trees to prevent their felling), and that they were ready for a new campaign against the ZhongRong proposals. Some expressed dismay that after having fought against a far less destructive proposal, something even worse appeared to be landing from on high, and generally any statement that bashed the Mayor or the developer received a hearty round of applause.

It was an eye-opening event, as I hadn't really prepared myself for the fact that committed, strongly active groups of local campaigners like that still existed in the apparently atomised 21st century. However, while I expected that there would be a fight, perhaps a number of legal challenges, I did think that the momentum of development and the political backdrop of the time would mean that the development was going to go ahead regardless. It seemed to me, however, that there was no way the development as it was envisaged could succeed, so I comforted myself with the thought of the new Crystal Palace being as much of a lost, empty, and melancholic environment as its predecessor had clearly ended up.

#

ZhongRong Group had been given an "exclusivity agreement" on the site at the top of the hill, meaning that all other development options were off the table while the details of the new proposals were thrashed out. This agreement was due to expire in February 2015, meaning that the negotiations and proposals were meant to wrap up and a planning application be made by that time. I and many others waited with bated breath to see what would happen, but no information was really forthcoming. No new architects' proposals were leaked out, no visualisations or press releases, it was officially the case that everything was still being negotiated. The website for the scheme, which had been regularly updating the progress of the open days and outreach events in the early months, had its last news update on 1st April 2014, going silent thereafter. Eventually, in late 2014, Johnson (who had already by this point lined up his safe seat for a return to the House of Commons), effectively admitted that things had stalled, euphemistically mumbling that "There are some concerns about the deliverability of the project".[23]

The exclusivity agreement eventually expired, and only then did the farcical nature of the process become clear. Bromley, as mentioned before, are a Tory-led council, and were clearly keen for the development to go ahead, considering the relatively large costs that were required for the park's upkeep and the incomplete and declining qualities it had. But in disgust, they eventually made publicly clear what they had been up against from their development partner. As the exclusivity agreement had been coming to an end, negotiations began on whether to set up an extension. ZhongRong Group communicated that they would only extend the exclusivity deal if the council signed a "revised lease document", subject to a number of demands.

The developer had only been offered control of the "top site" of the park, i.e. the location of the original palace itself. But they demanded that they be given control of the entire top half of the park. They demanded that they be exempted from seeking planning permission, and that all building would be at their own discretion. They wanted to take no part in the future maintenance or management of the park, indeed they wanted to take no responsibility for the costs that the council had incurred during previous negotiations (which were estimated in excess of £100,000). The developer wanted a 125-year-long lease on the site, which would be extended to 500 years when certain acts of Parliament were revised. And finally, the developer wanted their business plan to be kept secret from the public, and to be completely non-negotiable.

There is a possibility that this was a final slap in the face to the council and to Johnson, a set of ludicrous demands made as the developer was already walking out of the door. But even before these details were made public there were mumblings in the press regarding the impossible and illegal demands being made by the developer. It seems quite clear that this was a dangerous close shave, with Johnson making some kind of promises to people who held an attitude towards development that disregarded even the meagre concessions to the public good that are currently in place. The sheer gall of insisting that there was no need for the developer to get involved in the national planning process for a building of such vast size and impact suggests a total disregard for any kind of norms, or any consciousness of the historic context in which this apparently historic project was to occur.

At this point the main parties basically walked away, and the park today remains mostly as it was. A large lottery grant was lost during the exclusivity agreement, meaning that many of the works to the park that were meant to go ahead at that time were left stalled. However, the local campaign to raise the funds to make the subway safe for access is getting towards its goals, and certain parts of the terraces beneath the palace are being repaired, but the overall limbo has returned. London is lucky to have been spared the embarrassment of such a ridiculous project being foisted upon it, although when grilled at the end of 2014, Johnson was adamant that "I'll accept all criticisms. What I won't accept is the criticism that we're doing the wrong thing by stimulating economic activity in areas of London that have been stalled for a very long time."

"It will create a stunning oasis of tranquillity in the heart of our city"

The Garden Bridge

While Johnson stood chortling away on the terraces of Crystal Palace Park in late 2013, another of his hare-brained schemes was about to be revealed, one which — yet again — had been brewing for a lot longer than would first be let on. On 30th October 2013, the public were treated to the latest press event marking the launch of an organisation called the Garden Bridge Trust. The trust, which would soon be registered as a charity, was devoted to one purpose — the creation of a new river crossing over the Thames.

Was this, perhaps, the long-awaited crossing to the east, where it has been needed for at least half a century? The cable car had dodged that question completely, so perhaps now there was an opportunity to show that the real needs of London were being considered? But no, here the neglected part of the city that was to benefit from an increase in cross-water connectivity was the area around Temple, a desperately ill-connected backwater right in the centre of London, whose nearest bridge is all of 150 metres away.

Yet again, the announcement appeared to bypass completely any notion of preliminary work, tenders, competitions, and so on. Instead, the public were being introduced to another fully formed vision, insulated from the public purse — of course! — through the promise of private funding to come. And the cast of worthies was all present and correct — alongside Johnson was Richard Di Cani, the TfL executive who had been a driving force behind the sponsored cable car, while the concept for the bridge was attributed to celebrity actor and campaigner Joanna Lumley, not exactly known for her long track record in delivering transport infrastructure. Famous landscape designer Dan Pearson was roped in, and once again rounding off the gang was Thomas Heatherwick.

To be fair, it would be virtually impossible for someone like Heatherwick, running a business like Heatherwick's, to turn down such prominent, juicy opportunities as Johnson was throwing his way, but by this point there were ominous signs already visible. At the end of 2013 the buses were yet to be rolled out, so hadn't had the chance to be technically embarrassing, but there were still questions being asked about the quality or necessity of the new Routemasters. But in the middle of the 2013 Heatherwick had his name in the headlines for not very positive reasons, as he had become embroiled in the plagiarism case regarding the Olympic Cauldron. Another eggy face for him, but even as this began rumbling, here he was again, his alchemical design magic being associated with a project right from the very beginning.

So what was this "Garden Bridge" that was being launched? Essentially it was a 350-metre-long footbridge, with the gimmick of being topped by an expansive garden. It would be an "enchanted space in the middle of the busy city", it would "frame and enhance views of the iconic landmarks of London", and it would become "a cherished part of London's landscape". The design that Heatherwick had developed was based upon springing the bridge off two columns across the 350-metre-wide span. The bridge would be widest at these points, wider than any of the road bridges nearby, but would narrow the further away it got from the springing points, something like a warped mushroom.

The inventive Heatherwick magic in this case was mainly manifest in dividing the form of the bridge into a series of copper strips, a motif similar to one that he'd used in various places before, most notably the East Beach Cafe, a smaller project from earlier in his career. These strips would appear to fold out from the two main columns, referred to as "planters", with a concrete structure hidden within to take the weight of all the earth and organic material. The strips would create a folded edge to the bridge, which one commentator described as providing multiple opportunities for a "prow of the Titanic"[24] moment, a serrated profile with hundreds of corners to lean against.

Across the bridge, there would be a use of different bricks as paving to give a warm garden feeling, while the planting strategy would "reflect the development of cultivation and culture within London over the centuries", ranging from, apparently, "pioneer" at one end to "cultivated" at the other. Whether that meant anything whatsoever is moot, but all the visualisations showed a reasonably leafy environment, a bit worrying considering the tendency of CGI artists to over-green their work — if this was how green they expected it to be, how far short would the reality fall? How would it look on a rainy day in February?

This "wow factor" concept was fair enough, a little shallow perhaps, but the design of the bridge began to really fall apart at the ends. The proposed access points were over the lightly used Temple underground station to the north, and from a rather more busy part of the riverbank to the south, a route which is heavily walked by tourists passing between Tate Modern to the east and the Southbank Centre to the west.

One of the problems of pedestrian bridge design is that contemporary regulations require them to be accessible to all, but at the same time they need to reach a certain height to clear whatever it is they are spanning. The Millennium Bridge designed by Fosters and ARUP, built about a kilometre to the east on an axis with St Paul's Cathedral and the Tate Modern, is lucky in that it springs from an elevated position to the north, but at the south it has to awkwardly fold backwards on itself to reach the ground properly. But Heatherwick's design didn't even attempt to achieve this semi-successful model. Instead, the bridge design runs more or less flat to either end, at which point it actually has to encounter city infrastructure.

It's at this point that Heatherwick's not being an architect shows itself. The bridge, in the crudest of fashions, was designed to simply stop and plug directly into a set of stairs and a lift shaft, which would connect onto raised terrace platforms that would then lead back down to ground level. These terraces were described as "new pieces of public realm", but were actually about providing space to control access during busy times (i.e.

providing queueing space) but also to create open spaces that would be part of the land controlled by the Garden Bridge operator.

The landing points were referred to as "catalysts for future change", which, when translated from business euphemism, means being commercially exploitable spaces. To the north the bridge was proposed to land on top of Temple Station, an already-existing space that is currently open but under-utilised, with some concrete pavers and wooden benches. This would instead be transformed into a private space that could be rented out for events.

At the south landing, however, the bridge springs from an open space, so the design called for a large entrance pavilion to be constructed, again with restricted entry points, and with space for events and rent inside. This would take up a large amount of area from the walkway along the Southbank, and would in fact involve the felling of more than twenty existing trees that populate the area, which is of course ironic considering the whole raison d'être of the bridge.

The actual need for a structure like this was completely spurious. There was a great deal of talk of connectivity, but the fact remains that the Temple area to the north is quiet, an institutional rather than touristic area, and one which ironically is already known for its secluded gardens and quiet repose from the bustle of the city. There's no real demand for travel between the two banks, let alone travel that isn't already served by the many other bridges in the vicinity. The bridge is an attraction, pure and simple, another bauble for the Johnsonian Christmas tree.

Heatherwick's design takes a structure normally notable for its refinement and engineered qualities, and bloats it, filling it with concrete and soil and then cladding it in a metal sheath, a similar logic to the billowing throat of the Aquatics Centre, again removing the sense of work and labour that comes with the notion of expressed structure, and instead creating an iconic form entirely suited for a more spectacular understanding of architecture's purpose, to be seen in glossy photographs from in-flight magazines, to become part of the visual brand of a location. The Garden Bridge could be photographed with St Paul's Cathedral or the Houses of Parliament visible in the background, which would just add to the spectacle of it all.

It's working for Heatherwick though. Later research began to shed light on the murk that shrouded his initial engagement on the project. It would seem that his name was effectively tied to the bridge from a point long before the initial announcements, with freedom-of-information requests showing that he was basically the chosen designer, even while the motions were gone through considering tenders from Marks Barfield and Wilkinson Eyre, the usual suspects to receive insincere calls from the Johnsonian juggernaut. Like many of Johnson's murky behaviours, this information came to public knowledge mainly thanks to digging by committed journalists, such as the ongoing investigations undertaken by the *Architect's Journal*'s Will Hurst, who has performed a vital investigative role over the last few years.

Even though the Garden Bridge remains unbuilt, Heatherwick's other London projects are already somewhat tainted, and he's lost much of the critical goodwill that helped sustain his early career. But despite this he's managed to keep moving out onto the world stage. He's completed a number of large architectural projects in the Far East, including a university building in Hong Kong, and has teamed up with ultra-successful happy-go-lucky architect Bjarke Ingels to work with Google, including on campuses in California and London. He's got a job in Kings Cross designing what is basically a shopping mall, albeit with some jazzed-up landscaping, and, intriguingly, he has a commission for another garden over water, this time in New York.

Heatherwick's NYC project is another irony, considering first of all the uncertainty over whether his first one will actually occur, but also because the London Garden Bridge is, rather than some much-needed additional crossing, essentially the proposed solution to the problem of how London could match one of the world's most successful attractions in recent years, one itself located in NYC.

#

If London is to be considered as a global city, as we are so often encouraged to do, then it has to be seen as one of an archipelago of global city-islands, each related closely to each other, conceptually if not physically set adrift from the territories to which they are actually a part. Comparison metrics abound, from statistics of income and property value — whose citizens earn the most and have the biggest and most expensive houses? — to far more nebulous discussions of the kind you would find in *Monocle* magazine features: Which are the world's most liveable cities? Which city has the best croissants? The most exciting art scene? The most beautiful (and available) men and women?

As far as London is concerned, at least as far as the financial elite is concerned, it has been in an enviable position related to almost all European world cities, and has been able to tempt bankers and lawyers from all over the continent to partake of its ultra-high wages and bourgeois entertainments. London is consistently outperformed on the "liveability" tests, usually losing to Nordic cities like Copenhagen, but its real rivalry for elite attention is not with somewhere like Frankfurt, but with New York. For decades the question of where the epicentre of the financial world is to be found has been a tug of war between the City of London and Wall Street, and whichever answer you get has been a complex factor of the location of headquarters, the number of employees, and the sheer amount of money that passes through the computer terminals there.

But only a generation ago, both New York and London were thought to be basket cases, their global financial power shackled back to inner cities that had been depleted and emptied out of wealthy residents. In the late 1970s New York went bankrupt, while inner London was filled with squatters and derelict properties. Both cities were infamous for their apparent dangers, the failed housing estates, the drug addiction and criminality, and the racial and class struggles that underpinned these questions.

But both are famous for their later renaissance, the apparent transformation of NYC — often attributed to the harsh justice policies of Mayor Rudolph Giuliani —

from a Gomorrah into a safe entertainment metropolis, and the resurrection of the inner areas of London. Both benefited from thriving cultural industries, from the appearance of new kinds of bourgeois urbanites (the "hipster" being the best-known case in both), from booms in restaurant culture and other forms of experience commerce. Both saw young affluent residents move into areas they had been absent from (Williamsburg, say, or Shoreditch), with the ensuing discussions of cultural gentrification somewhat masking the underlying questions of rising land and property value: both now have a stunningly debilitating housing crisis.

Ken Livingstone's term as Mayor of London saw him claim leadership of the rivalry, as the banking sector in London threatened to become larger than that of New York, and with its tourism sector also recording a turnover well above that of NYC's. Part of this was due to more relaxed banking regulations in the UK, which in a globalised market is enough to bring anyone along for the ride, and to a very qualified extent the city as a whole benefits from the extra money that is sloshing around, at least in terms of the availability of small-plate dining.

But New York definitely had the edge with its urban environment. The 20th-century landscape of Manhattan is an attraction that London cannot hope to compete with, the world-famous ragged-toothed silhouette of capitalist skyscrapers far more exciting than the isolated Victorian nicknacks of the Houses of Parliament and Tower Bridge, or the English Baroque dome of St Paul's. Walking through London, you are often moved to feel a certain pity for the Chinese tourists, as the level of spectacle provided by the London urban environment is strangely underwhelming, its skyscrapers small by world standards, its classical architecture rudimentary and often less than half as old as it might first appear.

And yet the tourists still come. Perhaps some of this precarity of spectacle influenced Johnson over the years, with his desperation for architectural confetti to disperse across the capital, as if somehow at some point there would be an emperor's-new-clothes moment, and the world would realise that London is a scrappy mess of a city, all false decorum and barely concealed spivvery, deserving of little of the reputation it holds. And for the kind of project that would captivate Johnson, New York provided an exemplar.

Almost no project in the world since the millennium offers such a vision of the contribution that infrastructural spectacle can provide to a city's "improvement" as New York's High Line. By the end of the 20th century, this short spur of elevated freight railway, running through neglected parts of Chelsea and the Meatpacking District in Manhattan, was in line for demolition. Serving a function no longer required, it was just one of any number of structures to be swept away as part of the endless reinvention of Manhattan's abstraction. But as the new millennium dawned, a new sensibility was on the rise, and a burgeoning taste for the aesthetics of urban ruination meant that the High Line was rediscovered, explored, and celebrated, and a "Friends of the High Line" organisation was set up to campaign for its retention as a public amenity.

The major precedent for the proposal was a park in Paris called the Promenade Plantée, an urban park on ex-railway lines that opened in the mid-1990s, some of which runs along an old viaduct. But in the early 2000s, as the mood in New York changed after the September 11th attacks, the High Line idea snowballed, received the backing of Michael Bloomberg, the Mayor at the time, managing to raise $150 million from the state and various donors. Gradually, from 2006–14 the dilapidated ex-railway was transformed into a park, to designs by American architects Diller Scofidio & Renfro and landscape architects Field Operations. Their celebrated concept attempted to retain the beautiful post-industrial qualities of the High Line in its found state, with certain parts of track reinstated, paving designs that saw greenery creeping up through gaps, and a general planting scheme that drew from the hardiness of the plants that had managed to find their way there over the years.

The High Line was an immediate success, quickly becoming a world-recognised image of the regeneration of Manhattan, and its effects in terms of real estate and urban change. The area it passes through had been fashionable before, in the tradition of light-industrial space being converted into artists' studios and so on, but since the opening, the millions of pedestrians that pass along the park every year have seen a building boom unfold, with hotels, apartment blocks, major art galleries, super-tall towers, and other developments sprouting up with ridiculous regularity. Property values have soared in the vicinity, with the High Line often credited with transforming the entire area.

This process has become a large part of the mythology of the Bloomberg renaissance, the gentrification of an entire city, where previous dilapidation and danger all become part of the historic character, a sheen of differentiation marking the location out from all the other leisure and entertainment districts in all the other cities. It's a new development beyond previous generations, where now the non-place of malls and other suburban entertainment landscapes are seen as chronic and damaging. In the 21st century, the commercial leisure landscapes have reappeared in the inner cities, utilising a veneer of history and "grit", despite their fundamental similarities across the world, their monopolisations, their restricted imagination, their limits on possible activities, their increasing functional homogeneity.

Obviously, if you were Johnson, you'd think London needed a High Line. Something that could take some dilapidated and disused 20th-century space and turn it into a multiplier, a catalyst for development and regeneration, an attraction. For example, an absolutely perfect opportunity would have been the three-kilometre-long Kingsland Viaduct, a disused railway bridge that once led trains from Broad Street Station to Dalston, but had been closed down in the mid-1980s, near the height of East London's decline. Running through some of London's equivalently fashionable neighbourhoods, full of council estates, sprinkled with warehouse flats, galleries, and bars, I can recall looking down over its ruination from balconies at parties over the years. Turning this into a walkable park would have been a great chance to accelerate the embourgeoisement of areas like Shoreditch and Dalston, but the only problem was that it had actually been brought back into use as a railway line as part of the East London Line extension, opening in 2010.

If the most obvious candidate wasn't available, where else would be suitable? Johnson lent his name to a 2012 ideas competition held by the Landscape Institute, called A High Line for London, which would have been running at the same time as the discussions relating to the Garden Bridge were being firmed up. Much later, in 2015, a local proposal to turn a stretch of disused line in a newly fashionable neighbourhood of South London into the "Peckham High Line" was entertained by Johnson, who promised the measly sum of £10,000 towards the project, his mind on other things.

The Garden Bridge has to be seen, at least from Johnson's point of view, as London's direct answer to the High Line, but having to come up with a completely new environment due to the lack of derelict spaces to take over. The premise, of a semi-infrastructural green space, designed to function as an attraction that could be used as a development multiplier, is almost exactly the same. The promise, of an attraction that would bring in millions of visitors every year, with little harm on the public purse, was perhaps less so.

#

Johnson put his weight behind the Garden Bridge out of a thirst for something that would emulate the success of the High Line, but the idea itself had a much longer gestation period than even its secret development with Heatherwick would suggest. In fact, more than any other of the Johnsonian trinkets, the Garden Bridge is actually someone's brainchild, this someone being Joanna Lumley, a British "national treasure" who has used her friendship with Johnson and his weakness for unconventional approaches to push her dream right to the verge of construction.

Lumley has been in the public eye since the late 1970s, when she became famous as an actor in television series like *The Avengers* and *Sapphire and Steel*. A former model, born in India into a military family, her image was that of a dynamic yet traditional Englishness — she had both the swinging style of the libertine '60s and a very upper-class accent and poise. Her most celebrated role is as Patsy in the sitcom *Absolutely Fabulous*, playing a middle-aged fashion editor with a nihilistic drink problem, a satire on a very specific 1990s London social class of ageing party animals who resolutely refused to grow up and stop doing coke in the Groucho Club of a Wednesday evening.

Outside of this much-loved anti-hero, Lumley herself is an interesting character, using much of her time and resources for charitable activities, including a long-running campaign to achieve rights for the Gurkhas, and vocally supporting the Green Party and general environmental issues. She is fortunate in that she appeals both to conservative and progressive parts of the UK, her post-colonial poshness connecting with the *Daily Mail* readers and her cultural sophistication and good works to the *Guardian*-istas.

At the launch of the Garden Bridge in 2013, Lumley was credited with the overall concept, which might seem odd considering there is nothing linking her to the design or engineering professions. But it quickly became clear that Lumley's idea had a substantial gestation period. In 1999, two years after the death of Princess Diana in a car accident, Lumley received press coverage for an intervention in the process of selecting a memorial.[25] She campaigned against the idea, that would later become reality, of creating a memorial waterwork in Hyde Park, and argued instead that the memory of the People's Princess would be better served by a river-crossing memorial. She enlisted the help of engineers Arup, who would later be in the background of the Crystal Palace project, and went about trying to cost the scheme to around £19 million.

There were no real takers, but Lumley continued lobbying for the concept, intending to put it right at the point of the London Eye. By 2002 the project was already being described as a "garden bridge", but the Diana Memorial Fountain was opened in 2004 and the idea of a Diana bridge vanished, save for a satirical project by the architects FAT, who jokingly suggested carving the words of "Candle in the Wind 1997" into the flanks.[26] However, it would appear that Heatherwick had already by this point become associated with the project, through an introduction to Lumley.[27]

It seems that Lumley and Heatherwick properly teamed up in early 2012 when they heard that TfL were open to proposals for new river crossings over the Thames. Here, Lumley moved into lobbying mode, and a letter she sent to Johnson — whom she apparently has known since he was a child — was later revealed through a freedom-of-information request, and spoke of:

A thousand congratulations on being re-elected Mayor of London — our cheers and shouts reached the rafters, soared above the Shard — wonderful news for London! Thomas Heatherwick and I would very much like to meet you in the near future to talk most earnestly about the idea of a bridge, a great pedestrian bridge with cycle tracks along with container-grown trees: and beauty and practicality in equal measure.[28]

More investigations would show that Johnson met Heatherwick before the announcement of the project,[29] all giving the impression that the whole thing was stitched up from the start, and that a large piece of infrastructure, to be paid for largely out of the public purse, which would have to be subject to all manner of procurement rules, was yet again being elbowed into position through personal connections and secret meetings.

In a way, it's not really Lumley's fault — she had a dream, and her fortuitous connections and privileged position have allowed her to follow up on that dream, and her charm and passion for the project have, when combined with the pliancy of the Mayor, allowed her dream to come within a whisker of becoming reality. But it shouldn't need saying that this is not how things should work, that the public purse should not be seen as a piggy bank to be raided when one's friends come to ask for favours, and that jobs should not be given to people who happen to be attached from the beginning. The intentions may well be good, but the basic effect is cronyism.

#

Of all of Johnson's pet schemes the Garden Bridge has been the most controversial from the outset, and has sprouted a number of protest campaigns, ranging from those trying to uncover abuses of planning and procurement processes, others more concerned about the cost and pointlessness of the object, and others who are more concerned about the vision of the public realm that it represents.

For although Livingstone's public-space improvements were based around the genuinely public realm, London under him and increasingly under Johnson has seen the triumph of the privately owned public space. This is an area in a private development that appears to be open to all, but remains private land entirely, across which the public can only cross with the permission of the landowner, typically in somewhere like London an asset-management company such as British Land or Land Securities. While day to day this distinction might not be apparent, the ability to use these semi-public spaces can be revoked at a moment's notice, as was found out in 2011 when Occupy London attempted to set up their camp in Paternoster Square, a semi-public space owned by Mitsubishi Estates, who duly had the protesters legally thrown out. The objection to the Garden Bridge from this direction is that it represents an advanced form of this kind of commodification and enclosure, the creation of private gardens as attractions in a space that, in the form of the river, open air, and views of landmark buildings, is currently a public good.

The most prominent campaign that has been run against the Garden Bridge is that of Will Jennings, who has vigorously opposed the scheme through his "Folly for London" project. His catalogue of objections are worth following, as they present a smorgasbord of the different ways in which Johnson's projects have diminished London. For Jennings, the proposal for the Garden Bridge has shown no concern for public demand, instead proposing a private space to be paid for with public money. Like other Johnson attractions it will require massive maintenance costs, with profit going private but losses being paid for by the public. It serves no transport purpose, destroys existing views along the Thames, and actually involves the destruction of mature trees to create its own semi-green space. But most of all, it is entirely undemocratic, an unfolding process that we, the public, can only seem to watch as it is foisted upon us and we pick up the costs.

And this, at heart, is what is at stake in all of this. Each of these projects is, in their own way, profoundly contemptuous of the public, whether that be in the taking of public funds, or the taking of public space, or the overriding of procedures designed to protect the private interest. It's as though politics is just a game, played by the elites and those that they give access to, whether that is the ultra-rich, celebrities, or elite artists and designers, with the rest of us simply the mob, particles in a cloud of ambition that leads only to gratification for the people who think they belong at the centre of the world.

FOLLY

"A horse is a safer bet than the trains"

Transport in Johnson's London

A familiar sight in London, albeit one that I never myself had the chance to savour, was to see Johnson, fully suited, bedecked in a helmet of a colour marginally more fluorescent than his own hair, trundling his way between City Hall and his townhouse in Islington on a humdrum old street bike. As one of London's most famous citizens, and a cyclist, it was inevitable that Johnson would be one of the most high-profile cyclists in the city, the sight of his rumpled shirt and tie flapping around in the wind helping him portray himself as not quite a toff, or at least a toff not prone to extravagances. A particularly popular pastime for Londoners throughout his time as Mayor was to yell obscenities at him as he wobbled past, which by all accounts he would take in typically good humour.

But even as a regular cyclist himself, Johnson never really found the time to make an effort on cycling. When the lists are compiled, facetious as they are, a typical feature of cities considered to be particularly "liveable" is the thriving condition of their cycling culture. Copenhagen is often seen as the world's cycling capital, with nearly half its commuter journeys made by bike, taking advantage of favourable traffic rules and an extensive infrastructure, not to mention a reputation for stylishness. Indeed, the sight of thousands upon thousands of healthy and happy-looking people gliding swiftly through the classic European bourgeois streetscapes of Copenhagen or Amsterdam feels a civilisation away from the increasingly smoky grubbiness of London's streets.

London does have its cycling culture, one that is growing, but it can be a fraught and difficult one. Cyclists and drivers often seem to be engaged in a low-intensity war, with videos periodically surfacing, taken from the helmet-mounted cameras of cyclists, showing irate drivers physically attacking their wheeled counterparts. Motorists often accuse the cyclists of disregarding road rules and safety (or not paying road taxes) while cyclists cite a total disregard for their right to use the road safely.

The bike scene in London can often seem rather hardcore, taking some of its cues from courier culture — fixed-wheel bikes, high speeds, and risky road behaviour, with recent years seeing this disseminating into a significant aspect of white middle-class hipster culture. There is a curious situation whereby many Londoners seem comfortable spending large sums on a fashionably advanced bike, but then treat the preposterously high rate of bike theft as just another kind of inclement weather London is prone to.

But the main factor that makes London cycling seem unattractive is its lack of safety. The regularity with which news comes in of yet another cyclist killed under the wheels of a lorry is truly shocking, and yet people seem almost completely resigned to it. Over the last generation an average of almost twenty people a year have been killed in bike accidents, with far larger numbers of accidents resulting in injury. Street corners throughout the city are frequently adorned with "ghost bikes", painted white, covered in flowers, memorials to someone who died at that crossing. Over the years I've lived here I have attended the funeral of one person who died in a cycling accident, and I have witnessed a number of non-fatal crashes.

The primary danger for cyclists in London is a heavy vehicle, turning left. Any cyclist who is moving to the inside of a lorry that suddenly turns has almost no possible way to avoid going underneath, a situation made more dangerous when there are pedestrian barriers to the side of the road. In fact, during the construction boom, vehicles going to and from building sites made up a large proportion of the heavy vehicles on London's roads, and have been involved in a high number of serious accidents over recent years.

The perception of the risks posed by articulated buses was one of the reasons people were receptive to Johnson's campaign to bring back the Routemaster, and this, combined with his own cycling behaviour, might incline one to think that Johnson as Mayor would have been a champion of cycling safety. But at the same time he had to represent his natural constituency of motorists, the section of society that would be most put out by an increase in cycling lanes, restrictions on traffic mobility, and general preference given to non-motor transport.

It's not a great surprise, then, that Johnson's record on cycling was pretty poor: "superhighways", instigated by Livingstone, that were nowhere near substantial enough when implemented; a lack of any commitment to safety campaigns; a general acceptance of the status quo, as if the effort to make a difference on this front was beyond him. He was heavily criticised after appearing to blame the behaviour of cyclists for a particularly disastrous period of deaths in 2013,[30] even after he had earlier in the year finally moved forward with proposals to properly improve cycling conditions across the city, appointing a cycling commissioner and promising funds.

But there was one particular cycling project that Johnson managed to take on in his first term, one of the first built objects that would really be properly associated with him, and his first taste of the possible glory he could take from it, not to mention one of the first opportunities he had to cover up a large cost to the public purse through sponsorship.

In the later years of the Livingstone mayoralty, a scheme for short-duration bicycle hires was proposed, in imitation of a successful scheme that had been implemented in Paris a few years previously. This was developed to become part of the TfL landscape of provision, with a network of hiring stations, effectively electronic bike racks, to be deployed on pavements around the centre of the city. This would be a substantial undertaking, with construction works to take place on streets, the network and charging system to be designed, the IT systems to be planned, and of course the bikes themselves to be designed and purchased, all of which came out at a budget of around £140 million.

Johnson enthusiastically pushed the scheme forwards, apparently sensing that long before his buses were rolled out it would be an opportunity to have something tangible, visible to everyone, that he had achieved. And in an apparent coup, he was able to announce a £25 million sponsorship deal from Barclays bank, presumably trying to wash their reputation clean in the wake of the financial crisis and scandals that were dogging them at the time, such as money laundering or Johnson's erstwhile ally Bob Diamond's multi-million-pound bonus at a time of abject failure. In a pre-emptive echo of what would happen a few years later with the cable car, Barclays were able to have the colour of the cycle-hire scheme altered from a turquoise blue/green to the bold blue of the Barclays logo.

The bikes, installed in 2010, were a great success for Johnson — soon after their installation they became known as "Boris Bikes", a name that is still in use a year after he left office, and they allowed him to bask in the reflected glow of a progressive infrastructure project. But issues that would later dog his other projects were already clear at this early point. Financially, the sponsorship deal, now taken over by another bank, Santander, recolouring the bikes and roundels bright red, is worth roughly £5 million a year, and the hiring scheme has been recently bringing in approximately £10 million a year. But this income is offset against operating costs that reached £26 million in 2015/16, meaning that TfL has been and will presumably continue subsidising the scheme for more than £10 million every year.

#

Of all the major strategies and policies that were implemented during the eight years under Livingstone, one of the most significant in terms of day-to-day life was the improvement to the buses. Throughout the years when there was no specific London authority, the public-transport system, especially the buses, was perceived as a shambles, one of the main signs of the suburban disregard of the Tory government to urban life. From 2000, however, Livingstone integrated fares with the introduction of the Oyster Card system, created more bus priority lanes, improved timetables and maps, upgraded countdown indications, gave free fares to those aged 11–18, greatly improved night bus provision, and influenced a number of different improvements. This had the effect of almost doubling passenger numbers, turning the London bus network into something befitting a city of London's size.

Johnson's administration didn't turn these transport policies on their head, keeping most of the strategies inherited from Livingstone, but he simply didn't do much to continue the improvement. Bus use flattened out in London in 2008, which we might suggest may be related not just to the financial crisis but also to the political and financial priorities of the Mayor's office. In the years after Johnson took office, the large increase in service provision for the bus network came to an almost complete halt, despite the continued increase in London's overall population.

This decision not to improve matters meant that the buses have gradually been put under increasing strain, becoming busier and more crowded. But despite this lack of service improvement, the standard bus fare, 90p when Johnson took charge, was raised to £1.50 by 2015, an increase of two thirds in less than a decade. Johnson was widely criticised for these large increases, but they were at least partially caused by the gradual removal of government funding for TfL, as part of the 2010–15 austerity coalition, which made the London transport budget far more heavily reliant on income from fares.

But Johnson was at the same time raiding the TfL coffers to pay for his trinkets, with the budget having to stump up sums for the New Bus for London, the Thames cable car, and of course the Garden Bridge. Without these hundreds of millions of pounds being spent, some in lump sums, some in ongoing costs, there would not have been such need to continually increase fares whilst also letting services run down.

#

Despite Johnson's scrabbling for attractions, London does have its fair share of extant icons, but the vast majority of these speak of a certain historicist tendency. The UK has traditionally been reticent when it comes to the question of the aesthetics of modernity, and as the first nation to industrialise, the relationship between modernity and tradition is especially fraught here. In London's case, many of its most famous icons date from the Victorian era, perhaps exemplified by Tower Bridge, whose massive engineering works are hidden behind the most ludicrous historicist folderol.

But London gave the world one particular modernist symbol that anywhere in the world would be proud of. As the very first underground urban railway system, the London Tube has always been associated with a certain kind of modernity, but in the early 20th century, as nostalgic suburbia was extending out into the countryside, the left-wing commercial manager of the

Underground Group, Frank Pick, commissioned a visual identity for the Underground that has become one of the all-time design classics. The process started off with the "bullseye" roundel design, which was soon accompanied by the Johnston sans-serif typeface for signage, and later would include Charles Holden's designs for the London Underground headquarters and a series of stations on the Piccadilly Line. Finally, with Harry Beck's 1933 Tube map, the genial modernism of the Tube set the standard for all other underground systems, and indeed paved the way for the now near-global standard of rationalised navigational information systems.

Overall, the Tube under Johnson was one of the things that he played particularly safely, just enough to avoid decline, but not enough to prepare for foreseeable problems that are appearing over the horizon. Once again, the sense of doing just enough for the task at hand was clear. But over this period, the sense of the Underground has changed rapidly, as more and more of the rail franchises around London have been brought under TfL control. To look at the Tube map now is to have almost no sense of the clarity and beauty of Beck's original, as it now groans under the weight of the expanded DLR, the Overground network, the Croydon tram network, and what is now called TfL Rail. This is all part of maintaining a large city, the need to keep the infrastructure adequate to the growth of potential workers and citizens, lest the entire system grind up and become a massive constraint on economic activity.

For example, TfL Rail is a commuter service that currently runs along existing tracks that will form part of the route of a new London line, long in gestation but finally commissioned in 2008, called Crossrail. Leading from Reading to the west to Shenfield in the east, Crossrail is intended to provide a regular, semi-fast route right across London, upping potential commuter numbers by over ten percent on current total amounts, thus seriously increasing London's capacity for growth in employment in the centre. It has involved digging twenty-two kilometres of brand new tunnels across London, from Paddington to Canary Wharf, at a massive cost of over £15 billion, putting the project way out of the reach of tinkering from the lowly Mayor.

Over the years since construction work began, Crossrail has affected the experience of London to a large degree. Trips past either end of the tunnelling works would allow you to see the boring machines, long trains of equipment connected to massive Lamprey-toothed mechanical mouths, basking in the evening sun, while at various times entire city blocks became no-go areas as intermediate holes were sunk. Those working on construction projects would occasionally encounter areas of the earth beneath the city that had been reserved for tunnelling work, and could not possibly have foundations sunk into them. Controversially, one of the most characterful areas of London, the area around Tottenham Court Road, home to musical-instrument shops, dive bars, clubs like the Astoria and G.A.Y., legendary "social clubs" that were apparently fronts for massive cannabis distribution, and a small community of Korean businesses, was completely swept away for Crossrail, to be replaced with generic and safe redevelopment now that the tunnels are done.

Johnson may have had to stand and watch as the rock and clay were dragged back out of the tunnels, but he did manage to leave his mark on the project in one particularly cringe-inducing way. From the cable car it's already clear how little respect Johnson had for the underground and its identity, the neat recuperation of giving easy corporate access to a design classic whose original reason for existing was to differentiate the communications of the underground from all the commercial detritus of the Edwardian city. But in early 2016, not long before he left office, Johnson proudly announced that his idea to rename Crossrail "The Elizabeth Line" was to come true.

While it is the case that London is plastered in royalism, including in the form of the Underground's Victoria and Jubilee Lines, the sheer embarrassment of this strange deferential informality (Victoria at least has a period named after her, whereas Crossrail won't even be called Elizabeth II), combined with its queasy purple colour scheme, feels like an affront from the old boy, forcing us all to curtsey whenever we enter this most modern of rapid transit systems. It was probably just another of Johnson's endless series of whims, calculated to rub some statesmanlike sheen onto him as he got ready to launch for the top job, but it feels more like just another stupid idea that we're all going to have to live with for as long as we stick around.

Overall, the Tube handles well over a billion journeys a year, and is easily the most important organ of the metropolis, completely vital to its functioning. Johnson knew from the beginning that there was no chance for him to take risks with the Tube, but it was also the source of one of his biggest challenges, a conflict with a personality who for once matched his own in terms of force and drive, one that threatened to throw Johnson's much-downplayed elitism into sharp relief.

Born in 1961, Bob Crow was three years older than Johnson, and had been head of the Rail, Maritime, and Transport Workers Union (the RMT) since 2002. A proper Essex boy from Epping, the very last station on the Central Line, he had had an uneasy relationship with his ostensible ally Livingstone, due to the aggressive tactics he pursued in industrial negotiations, tactics which nonetheless had made him very popular with the members. With Johnson at City Hall, and then later with the Tories back in power, Crow was one of the most prominent men of the Left in the whole of the UK.

Crow's tactics for the RMT were robust, and he had no qualms about using the threat of strike action. On a number of occasions after 2008 his members walked out, meaning the Tube could barely run, causing huge economic damage as people struggled to travel around the city. Many of the strikes were called in response to planned redundancies, such as Johnson's infamous plan to close down ticket offices across the network after making an election promise not to do exactly such a thing, but others were due to broken negotiations over pay and conditions.

In some ways the two men were almost exact opposites — not just in terms of class, but also in their attitude to the world. Crow was widely considered — even to enemies — to be selfless in his approach to his role, making all decisions based on the principle of fighting for the advancement of his members, whereas the one thing that everyone can agree on about Johnson is that there is literally no greater goal for him than the accumulation of power for his own enjoyment. But these reflections were further mirrored by the way Crow was regularly dragged through the mud for earning £150,000 a year while living in a council house, whereas Johnson's lifestyle was thought of as frugal despite his multi-million-pound townhouse and the hundreds of thousands of pounds a year he was paying in school fees for his children, not to mention his infamous description of £250,000 a year for his *Telegraph* column as "chicken feed".

The two mirrored personalities were even linked by parallel appearances on *Have I Got News for You*, where Crow's refusal to take his political hat off made him come across as joyless and unfunny compared to the disarming buffoon routine so instrumentalised by Johnson. But despite all this they never met, with Johnson continually refusing to directly negotiate with Crow, perhaps reasoning that here was someone who finally was as cunning as himself, and who therefore risked showing him up in a way he couldn't bear to accept.

Crow's tactics for the RMT exposed one of the rawest edges of political sentiment in contemporary Britain, a resentment described as "negative solidarity", as in "I suffer, so I don't see why anyone else should have nice things". The London public, when asked, usually express highly negative opinions on the actions of the RMT, especially with regard to strikes, and around the time of industrial action many people are comfortable with voicing the opinion that the drivers should be killed, preferably by throwing them in front of their own trains. The fact that Tube drivers are paid more than £50,000 a year makes many people upset, and I've certainly had to listen to people explain that the good working conditions of some Tube workers are the main reason why they shouldn't be allowed to take industrial action, rather than a demonstration of the basic efficacy of such a tactic!

The more serious objection is that the RMT are in a very privileged position, in that their own industrial action can create crippling disruption, far more than almost any other job. The spiteful accusation that they "hold Londoners to ransom" is to a certain extent the truth, but should be seen as a model of solidarity rather than an aberration to be stamped out as soon as possible. Crow's RMT were both the ideal of union activity in the current age, but also perhaps its limit, whose achievements were virtually impossible to replicate in any other environment.

But any chance of a proper reckoning between Johnson and Crow disappeared when Crow died suddenly of a heart attack on 11th March 2014. Johnson, rhetorician that he is, was magnanimous and gracious in his praise of the dead man,[31] but also could not have been unaware that one of his most impossible-to-subdue adversaries was now no longer able to put him on the spot.

#

Since the days when low-budget airlines started making use of the low berthing rates of out-of-town airports, London has had a number of airports to choose from. Planes fly from the hodgepodge of terminals at

London Gatwick situated to the south of the city, a half-hour's travel by train, and to the northwest is the dismal selection of shacks on a plateau that makes up London Luton. To the northeast lies Stansted, whose remarkably clear design by Norman Foster ushered in a new form of airport design for the mass travel age, but has now been comprehensively trashed by retail agents turning its vast abstract interior into a slalom course of tacky shops.

Two smaller international airports add to the available provision, with London Southend along the Essex coast to the east being improved and upgraded in recent years, while for those with business on the continent there is the ridiculous privilege of using London City Airport, flying low over the tops of the towers of Canary Wharf, waltzing effortlessly from the front door to the plane in what feels like seconds, with complementary copies of the *Financial Times* handed out next to a cafe whose lamps are shaded by suspended bowler hats.

All of these airports are dwarfed by London Heathrow, that extraordinary city-within-a-city, a vast landscape of taxiways and tunnels, roundabouts and runways, hangars, hotels, long-stay car parks and conference centres, covering an area of over twelve square kilometres. It employs more than 70,000 people, and 1,400 flights use the runways every day, the planes stacked up in three-dimensional traffic jams above the centre of the city.

More than seventy million people pass through Heathrow every year, which until recently made it the busiest international airport in the world. But recent years have seen Heathrow surpassed by both Dubai and Hong Kong, symbolic changes in centres of gravity, and ones that are bringing certain challenges to a head. Airport capacity is seen to be vital to economic functioning, and it has long been a concern that a restriction of airport capacity at Heathrow was adversely affecting the ability of London and the UK to do business with emerging economies and markets, and thus losing out globally.

The problem with Heathrow is that it is too urban — it sits within the M25 orbital motorway, and to its outskirts are large built-up areas of residential land. This inability to expand over the years partially led to the increases in traffic across the other London airports, but there are few options for expansion. Various government initiatives have been set up, most recently a set of white papers and consultations that looked into the various options. The main contenders were new runways at either Gatwick or Heathrow, and over recent years London commuters were bombarded with adverts recommending each of these options, and how they were the only solution to the capacity problem.

The eventual winner, recommended by the Airports Commission, and approved by the government in late 2016, was to expand Heathrow Airport with a new runway to the northwest, at an estimated cost of around £18 billion. While this was the clearest option, there were a number of major objections, including the increased noise and pollution from the vast increase in air traffic passing over Central London, the destruction of various areas currently home to wildlife, not to mention the destruction of the British Airways headquarters at Waterside. The wider objection that airport expansion runs counter to the absolute need to reduce carbon dioxide emissions didn't seem to find much traction overall.

Johnson's own position on the matter was typically strange, but typically self-aggrandising. It was basically shrewd for him to oppose the expansion of Heathrow, in the knowledge that it was probably a foregone conclusion, yet another case of him setting himself up to lose so that he could appear virtuous. But rather than going with the rival Gatwick, Johnson couldn't help but hitch himself to a wild scheme, one which had its own not-quite-illustrious history.

In the early 1970s, the UK government embarked upon an earlier study of the options for airport expansion in the London area, as Heathrow was already congested. In the ambitious and optimistic times, the answer was a remarkable concept, for a large new island to be constructed from the shallows of Maplin Sands off the Essex coast, completely avoiding resistance from existing urban areas. A new container port and settlement for airport workers, as well as a high-speed train link, would be constructed. Works had actually begun on the project, but it was quickly cancelled in the wake of the 1973 oil crisis.[32]

Johnson's own preference for the airport was a resurrection of this idea, now known as the "Thames Hub", which would involve a giant new peninsula being built on reclaimed land off the Isle of Sheppey, with four runways that would provide flight capacity long into the future. This idea, not so ridiculous in an age where airports are reasonably often constructed in this way, was seized upon by the press and nicknamed Boris

Island. Serious work went into it, including a fairly sizeable feasibility study put together by Foster and Partners, who designed not only Stansted but the island airport of Chek Lap Kok in Hong Kong, but it wasn't ever really taken seriously as a contender.

With Boris Island, Johnson was able not only to keep his profile up, but also to keep himself clean from the debates around Heathrow, managing to not offend the citizens by advocating something as far away from them as it was reasonably possible to get. But the thinking process was reminiscent of his general attitude, the frivolous option picked as it would make him look better, the genuine politics of reconciling so many different competing interests ignored in favour of a feel-good vision that was hard to fault, as long as it remained in the realm of imagination.

"I suppose with houses and assets, then I guess I would be a millionaire. But so are a lot of people."

Housing in Johnson's London

Returning back home in my first few years of living in London, I would always be asked "But isn't it really expensive?" Back then, as a young adult, visiting the capital would be seen almost as taking a city break to one of those expensive cities, where you'd take extra spending money for the entertainments, with one of the of the more celebrated things to despair over being the price of a pint — sometimes as much as £3!

Housing was a similar matter, and for as long as I've been alive it has been the common conception that London was filled with people for whom the price of a house was the most important topic of discussion that there could possibly be. Even events like the negative equity of the early 1990s were part of this London wealth game.

But looking back over the decades since the mid-'90s it's astonishing how little the conversation has changed, despite a near-constantly widening gap between the rich and the poor, an ever-larger discrepancy between the demand for housing and its availability (and the decreased options for alternative forms of living), and the stretching gulf between wages and rents.

.

In the mid-2000s the problem was already physically visible in the plethora of shiny multicoloured housing blocks that were going up across various parts of London, especially deprived city parts of East London that were being "rediscovered" by the middle classes. This was part of the bourgeois rediscovery of the inner city that was occurring across the developed economies, becoming tied up with the term "gentrification", and which was already considered a serious issue even before the financial crisis blew everything out of the water. In the first few years of living in London my response to the expense question was "It is, but you get paid more and it's overall worth it", while since the crash the only response can be a vaguely trapped "Yes".

If London already had a housing crisis, the financial crisis exacerbated this massively. The crash originated in the property market, and in the immediate aftermath many people were affected by mortgages and other loans being unpayable. Prices in new builds dropped calamitously, at the same time as many were repossessed. A particular block in Greenwich, called The Pinnacles, became a celebrated example after its flats lost half their value and a majority were taken back by the banks. It looked like the Blairite property dream might well be over.

This was the context into which Johnson entered as Mayor, a Tory under a Labour government. He discussed the crisis of affordability, honoured the difficulties of first-time buyers, and made a manifesto promise to deliver 50,000 affordable homes by 2011. It would still be another two years before there would be a Tory government in power across the whole of the UK, but Johnson's initial housing policy saw early examples of language that would later become very familiar, speaking of a "localist" agenda that would take planning power away from central authorities and, for example, allow local councils to set their own quotas for affordable housing.

The first few years after the crash saw a slump in construction, but compared to the rest of the UK the recovery in the property market was quick, in part because of the influx of foreign money into London property. In this context, the media became fixated on stories of the sufferings of the housing crisis, sometimes myopic and frivolous, such as the endless tales of the middle classes being forced into buying gigantic terraced houses along the Kent coast because they could no longer afford one in Notting Hill, or various inconsequential mutterings about "gentrification" and the accessibility of artisan foodstuffs.

But often the coverage of the crisis was shocking and vital, and could be described as Dickensian without much hyperbole. There were investigations that uncovered terrifying levels of overcrowding, often affecting migrant labour; there were exposés of the unscrupulous practice of creating "beds in sheds" for extortionate sums; there were the regular reports of eye-watering rent rises year on year. All this was occurring while the rich were able to double the value of their houses by digging down floors to create "mega-basements", while elsewhere whole developments were lying empty, a condition identified through analysing council tax records to see if there was anyone actually registered to live there at all, a phenomenon known as "buy-to-leave".

Clearly Johnson couldn't ignore this kind of situation, and there was an interesting manoeuvring act that happened as the new coalition government formed in 2010. This was the election on the concept of "austerity", when much of the British public agreed that it was indeed the government's fault that the economy had collapsed, and that, yes, a national economy was essentially similar to a household budget, with "means" that had to be "lived within", and finally that, yes, the way to get out of this whole mess was to stop spending so much money on frivolities like social welfare and local government.

Johnson and his team clearly knew that this was a recipe for disaster in London, home to some of the poorest areas in the whole of the UK but also the scene of almost the entire economic recovery, such as it was at that point. In July 2010, just months after the election, Johnson attempted to attain concessions from the government that the caps on housing benefit that they were introducing, which were predicted to throw tens of thousands of Londoners immediately into poverty, would only be introduced after a transitional period for adjustment.[33]

This was an interesting development. It showed Johnson's own independence in that he wasn't toeing the party line that others such as Iain Duncan-Smith were, that the austerity measures were immediately necessary. It also appeared to show a level of compassion that admittedly was rarely visible from Johnson but was never to be seen with George Osborne or Duncan-Smith. It showed that there was a mood to Johnson in the early years of the mayorship that was not entirely oriented towards the oiling of the gears of the rich, and that he was trying out a number of voices at that stage that he would largely later abandon.

But the housing crisis would be one of the main themes in London politics throughout Johnson's terms, and despite occasional bursts of positive rhetoric, his overall behaviour on this front was at best ineffective and at worst genuinely exacerbating. Johnson's basic strategy for the housing crisis was to have as many houses built in London as was humanly possible, and it certainly didn't really matter what they were. He'd promised 50,000, and he'd look like an idiot if he didn't make a dent in that.

#

Once upon a time in the UK, planning departments were a powerful and active force. In the post-war age, planners at all levels of government made large-scale plans for cities, including the Abercrombie Plan for Greater London that was formulated during the Second World War, and which was such an important factor in post-war construction. Furthermore, planning departments once developed the briefs for large local authority developments, analysing the sites and translating national policy into instructions for how many, and what type, of dwellings to build. Architects would design housing estates based upon densities that were predetermined, to the extent that it used to be reasonably common for reticent architects to be told by the planners that there was more demolition and construction to be done on a site than they themselves thought appropriate.

Planners also created visions of futuristic urbanism, such as the Buchanan Report of 1963 that became Traffic in Towns, which set out a vision for three-dimensional urbanism that segregated cars and pedestrians. London still bears the traces of this idea, as it was partially implemented in the "Pedway" scheme to create a series of raised walkways connecting the new developments of the area, which if fully implemented would have resulted in an entirely seamless upper level where one could walk without ever having to set foot at road level. The Pedways weren't developed to a great extent before the prevailing attitudes to urbanism rejected the three-dimensional city, meaning that it only exists as a series of disconnected fragments embedded into the sides of buildings, or in the relatively complete artificial topography of the Barbican Estate.

Nowadays, planning departments have a very different role to play. Since the crises of the 1970s and their Thatcherite resolution, not to mention the disillusionment caused by the apparent failures of modernist urban planning and social housing, planning departments have become largely reactive. Large-scale masterplans are still created, but currently the private developer is the main agent involved in the creation of new space. Today, the process basically involves the developer submitting an application to the local authority alongside a fee calculated on the proposed size of the development, which the planning department then consider and make a decision whether to grant permission. One of the major results of this kind of system is that rather than the planning department setting the brief, the developer will by and large attempt to get away with the largest development they possibly can, and the planning authority has to judge that against various policies and plans at local and national levels, including the London Plan set by the Mayor and the GLA.

This system should in theory work reasonably smoothly, without the dangers of planning departments adjudicating on schemes that they themselves have effectively prepared, and with guidance and policy clearly available for the developers to tailor their proposals to, but in recent years everything has gone a little off the deep-end. The London building boom has been a force encouraging developers to be more aggressive, and the "austerity"-led decimation of local authority budgets post-financial crisis has meant that planning departments are operating on nowhere near sufficient resources. This has all meant that the antagonistic character of the planning process has been skewed wildly in favour of the developers, with a number of examples of planning departments being completely outwitted by highly funded legal teams of developers, not to mention revolving doors being set up so that planners can then walk into lucrative jobs to come. Plans do exist, but it is well-known that it is possible to exceed or warp these through deft navigation of planning law.

While it is possible to argue that the London Mayor is a high-profile but low-authority role, planning is one of the issues over which Johnson had a serious amount of power. Any proposed development in London over a certain height, incorporating a certain amount of dwellings, or taking place in a sensitive location such as the green belt or a conservation area, was automatically referred to the Mayor's office. Any of these strategically important applications would receive comments from the Mayor before the local authority would then deliberate and make their decision, after which the application would return to the desk of the Mayor.

At this final point Johnson could do nothing, letting the decision stand, as mostly happened on the 130 or so applications that were referred to him. But he also had the power to automatically refuse a planning application, which he did on seven occasions. For example, an application to add facilities to London City Airport that the local authority had granted permission to was refused on the grounds of it contradicting aviation policy regarding noise and pollution, although we might ask whether "Boris Island" had anything to do with this decision. In another case, Johnson threatened to block the application made by Land Securities for the Victoria Site mentioned previously until they made a contribution towards the Crossrail tunnels that were being dug beneath their site: the developer complied and the buildings went ahead.

But Johnson also had the power to "become the planning authority" himself, a process that was known as "calling in". In this case, he would make a notification of his intentions, at which point he was obliged to hold a public hearing at City Hall to discuss the application in question, before making his own decision in writing. In theory this power is conceived in order to deal with the most significant applications, the construction of which would have major effects upon more than one local authority, or would affect the status and implementation of large-scale planning policies. Again, in theory this means that the Mayor could use this power to both refuse or grant permission to a development, but a closer look at his behaviour on this front speaks volumes.

Over the eight years of his mayoralty, Johnson "called in" nineteen separate planning applications, with a certain pattern emerging. For example, in August 2009, an application for Hertsmere House,[34] a residential tower of more than sixty storeys, was refused by Tower Hamlets Council due to its overwhelming size, and its effect on a conservation-area setting — the tower was to sit next to the Museum of London Docklands, contained in one of the only remaining Georgian warehouse buildings still left from the early days of the docks. Johnson called in the application, deciding to grant permission based upon the importance of maintaining Canary Wharf's prominence as a business centre, and accepting the absence of affordable housing in the scheme on the same terms.

This example was typical of almost all the applications that Johnson got himself involved in. An application to redevelop the site of gasworks in Southall[35] was refused by Ealing and Hillingdon Council in December 2009 for being far too large, an example of overdevelopment, but Johnson overturned this, as he did with Camden's decision in June 2011 to refuse a redevelopment of the "Saatchi Block"[36] for the same reasons, and as he did again at the Southwark Free School in June 2013,[37] and Alpha Square,[38] another gigantic residential tower in the vicinity of Canary Wharf.

Linked to the principle of "overdevelopment" were the attempts by councils to refuse planning permissions based upon the mix of tenures within the new developments. It has become common-sense knowledge that the phrase "affordable housing" is a cruel joke in London. Legally it refers to housing that is offered at a specific value that is 80% of the market rate for housing in the local area, but everyone knows that when the housing costs more than fourteen times the average salary, calling anything "affordable" is just salt in the wounds. But even so, councils attempt to set targets for the number of flats that are designated as "affordable" in any new development that is to be considered in their area, while developers use their legal resources and whatever sleight of hand they possibly can in order to reduce or eliminate that requirement, and in Johnson they had a helping hand.

A development for Trocoll House[39] in Barking and Dagenham was refused in part because the developer was proposing that the scheme included no affordable housing: Johnson gave the development permission. The City Forum[40] development in Islington was granted permission by Johnson after the council refused, arguing that the preponderance of small studio flats in the scheme were completely unsuitable for the actual demand for family housing in the borough, while Hackney Council was overturned after refusing a development at Holy Trinity Primary School[41] for being too large, for badly designed internal arrangements, and for issues of daylight.

There weren't just objections based on scale and tenure that Johnson was willing to override, however. A development called Eileen House[42] in Southwark became controversial in 2011 because of its proximity to the Ministry of Sound nightclub, which had been operating

across the road since 1991. The property crisis in London
has been such that available venues for nightlife have
been dwindling, victims of rising rents, stifling security
measures, a general drift away from hedonism amongst
the younger generation, but also a series of celebrated
cases where new residents in a neighbourhood make
noise complaints leading to the closure or strangulation
of long-established venues. The club and its many
supporters had been waging a campaign for a number
of years based upon the fear that any new residential
development near them would likely result in noise
complaints that would end their business. Johnson
called the scheme in, and gave permission, but in this
case also imposing serious noise-abatement measures
on the developer that would hopefully prevent such a
confrontation arising.

Elsewhere, Johnson went against his apparently
conservative credentials by granting permission to
developments that seriously clashed with local heritage
and historic urban fabric. A redevelopment of the
London Fruit and Wool Exchange[43] in Spitalfields was
heavily criticised not only for proposing to gut out the
innards of the building, leaving only the historic skin, a
design process known as "façadism", but it also involved
the demolition of an historic pub and other heritage
assets. Johnson waved it through.

Nearby, in the area known as Norton Folgate,[44] a
zone of 19th-century warehouse buildings, locals fought
a campaign against a scheme to transform it into offices
and workspaces. While it is true that the developers
had selected a group of some of the best architects in
the UK to work on the proposals, the site was to one

side of legendary Georgian Spitalfields, one of the most celebrated examples of British conservation, but also early gentrification, where richer whites moved into an area of dilapidated sweatshops and Bangla slums in the 1980s, restoring it to a late-18th-century glory that it never possessed at the time. Many of those who had been involved in this process campaigned against the Norton Folgate proposals, but these too were given the nod by Johnson.

Meanwhile, at the Bunhill Fields cemetery[45] where Daniel Defoe and William Blake are buried — a beautifully leafy and quiet oasis in the City of London, near where I once worked and of which a photograph still serves as the backdrop to my mobile-phone screen — a new block of housing was refused by Islington Council because of its detrimental effect on the setting of the Grade-I-listed burial ground, not just in terms of light but also for its impact on localised wind patterns. Johnson granted permission for the development not long before he left office.

The most extreme cases of Johnson's planning interventions were those that had not even reached the point at which the local authority had made a ruling, and where the actual applicant made a request for Johnson to intervene. At Convoys Wharf,[46] a huge site on the Thames in Deptford, a dock landscape overlaid with the remains of significant architecture and infrastructure going back to Tudor times, a development of nearly 4,000 homes has been proposed for over a decade since it stopped being used as a loading dock for the newspaper industry. Various different developers and architects have been involved, including News International and Richard Rogers, but the current scheme is proposed by Hutchison Whampoa and designed by Terry Farrell.

In October 2013, the developer wrote to Johnson, requesting that he took charge of the planning application, stating that "The point has been reached where the relationship between application and local planning authority seems to have broken down". Effectively, they knew that the scheme as they had designed it would be unacceptable to Lewisham Council, seeing as it consisted mostly of luxury housing of the sort that appeals on the international property market, and little to no affordable or social housing, despite being part of a highly deprived local area. Johnson duly took over, and in 2015 he granted permission to the development, as he also did with a proposal to redevelop the Westferry Printworks.[47]

#

Perhaps the most infamous example of Johnson's predilection for "calling in" planning applications has been the saga of the Mount Pleasant redevelopment. The proposals, counterproposals, campaigns and arguments that have raged over this site over the last few years have been a microcosm of the political struggles over what role the housing industry should actually be playing in society, what their responsibilities are, and for whose benefit they operate.

Mount Pleasant is located in Clerkenwell, along the route of the 38 bus, an area of Central London surprising for its folds and undulations, lying as it does across the valley of the Fleet River, which still gurgles away deep underneath the pavements. The site known as Mount Pleasant is best known for being the location of the UK's primary mail-sorting office, a huge neoclassical factory block mostly built in the late 1920s, which covers a vast area across half of the site. The other half, which was once the site of a Victorian prison, is a surface car park, constantly filled with the bright red vans of the Royal Mail. It is this openness that has led to the urban myth that the Mount Pleasant site is the last World War Two bomb site left undeveloped in Central London, a falsehood that nevertheless testifies to the appeal to developers of such a large open space in such a promising location.

For a long time now schemes have been conceived and planned for how to densify and develop the site, with the primary challenge being the maintenance of the Royal Mail operations throughout the development. For a long time, the sheer significance to the operation of the country that the Royal Mail represented meant that there could be no significant disruption to operations for any length of time, which made the whole prospect extremely difficult. One popular concept for a long time was to use the car park as the location for a phased construction of a brand-new mail centre, and when this was finally complete and operational, the original centre to the north could be demolished and redeveloped. In fact, one of my first jobs after moving to London involved a little work on this long-running scheme, although the logistical difficulties and sheer institutional inertia of the Royal Mail meant that the whole thing proceeded at a barely noticeable pace.

—

After the financial crisis, and with all manner of privatisations and restructuring of the Royal Mail, the rebuild option for redeveloping the mail centre was abandoned. Instead, the mail centre was to be upgraded gradually, and the car park to the south was to be the prime location for the redevelopment. A series of rationalisations, and presumably sell-offs, meant that the "bathtub" parking area to the north could be partially released, which would provide the opportunity to develop the site in earnest.

A planning application was submitted in June 2013 by Royal Mail Group, which outlined their proposals for the immediate Royal Mail site and another surface carpark site that they owned across the road. The architects that were employed were four stalwarts of the dependable mainstream architecture scene, Allies and Morrison, AHMM, Fielden Clegg Bradley, and Wilkinson Eyre. The proposals were to create a variety of new housing blocks, ranging from three to fifteen storeys in height, and in total containing nearly seven hundred new housing units, potentially worth at least £4 billion in sales at then-average local prices.[48]

The designs themselves were super polite, modern construction techniques draped in a skin of traditional-looking bricks, with order and detailing tailored to gently mimic the early-20th-century commercial buildings that surround the site (although not the heavy concrete facade of a large 1970s Richard Seifert building nearby, which is apparently a context not worth mimicking). It was basically a perfect example of contemporary British residential architecture, whose visual deference to locale and harking back to previous techniques belied its highly speculative and ruthless rationale.

It takes a huge amount of work to prepare a planning application for a development of that size, thousands and thousands of pages or reports, drawings and summaries, all condensed in a document called a "Design and Access Statement" prepared by the architects. The designs, the reports, the consultations, and a whole series of pre-application meetings and advisory documents are all intended to be as uncontroversial as possible, in order to smooth the way towards getting the opportunity to build and sell all these precious, precious flats.

As occurred on other major developments in London, Johnson was directly asked to take control of the Mount Pleasant application before the two councils on whose land the site sits, Islington and Camden, were able to make their original decision. The sticking point, such as it was, was once again the question of "affordable housing", in terms of, as the applicant put it, "the maximum reasonable amount of affordable housing that the project is able to sustain in the context of viability testing".[49]

This particular question needs a little explanation. A major part of any large contemporary development is the question of "viability". Essentially, the developer hires a consultant to analyse the projected build costs of the project, against the expected value of the space to be created, with a view to achieving a very specific level of profit across the whole scheme, typically 20%. Now of course this is exactly the sort of thing that a developer should be doing, seeing that their work is speculative, but in the current environment, and as a number of campaigning articles by Oliver Wainwright of the *Guardian* have amply shown, the Viability Assessment has become a tool that developers have used again and again to escape their responsibilities for the creation of affordable or socially rented housing.

The basic problem is that there is no transparency. Developers are able to claim that any requests for parts of the development to be given over to space that would be worth less than the market rate would put their schemes in jeopardy, and that they will have to walk away. Local authorities cannot afford the expertise to challenge this, or if they can, they have to hire consultants with blatant conflicts of interest, who cannot be trusted to give evidence against people who are the source of most of their income.

In the case of Mount Pleasant, the applicant cut their initial offer of 20% affordable down to 12%, despite the target of both local authorities being 50% affordable. They then claimed that Islington and Camden, by hiring a further independent consultant to analyse the applicants' viability assessments, were going back on previously issued advice, and could not be trusted to rule on the planning application reasonably. In effect, they were asking Johnson to say yes where the councils were likely to say no, based on the meagre amount of affordable housing being proposed, and the questionable calculations being used in the viability assessments. Johnson duly complied.

But this wasn't the end of the matter. In late 2015, after the application had been decided, a group calling itself the Mount Pleasant Association announced its intention to utilise a new planning law related to the government's "localism" agenda to attempt to get permission for their own scheme to be built on the site. The MPA was made up of a number of local residents who were dismayed by the scale of the proposed development, the "fortress"-like qualities of the massing, the mediocre and cynical architecture, and the tenure mix which they were worried would be bought by outside investors and left empty most of the time. Their intention was to lodge a "community right to build" application, which meant that if they could secure the funds they would be able to jump the queue when the sites came up for development sale, as the Royal Mail were planning to do.

The motives of the community campaigners are hard to criticise, and their main concern and selling point was that they wanted to prove that more affordable housing could be built on site, without necessarily creating developments of great mass and height. But in pursuing this direction they found themselves with some strange bedfellows. Their main ally in the process is a group called Create Streets, who bill themselves as a "non-partisan social enterprise and independent research institute" advocating traditional urbanism. The core idea that Create Streets have is based on the fact that when shown a picture of a nice house with a garden in the sun, and one of a concrete tower block in the rain, people will generally say they would prefer to live in the home with a garden.

From this banal observation, a whole host of urbanist ideas flow out: terraced housing is a better use of space than high-rise, it allows for adaptation, it allows for higher densities and lower build costs, it is more popular.

Again, these are more or less correct in certain cases, but it's the implications that come next where things start to get sinister. Create Streets argue that the modernist council estates of London contain more than 300,000 homes of types that people don't like, on sites that are under-utilised, and built at lower densities than the historic norm. In theory, if redeveloped, these sites could possibly accommodate an additional 200,000 homes, thus making the housing crisis much easier to solve.

This argument eventually found itself being turned into a report by property consultant Savills for the government in early 2016.[50] This argued that all the modernist council estates of London should be considered as "brownfield" land, meaning that they could be demolished and rebuilt according to principles of traditional (meaning late-18th-century) urbanism. This would unlock a huge amount of space to build huge numbers of extra homes, and the report was enthusiastically received in government.

If this sounds too good to be true, it's because it is. Despite their protestations of non-partisanship, Create Streets grew out of the right-wing think tank Policy Exchange, who have strong ties to various elements in the Tory party, including figures such as Michael Gove or the *Times*' Daniel Finkelstein. Create Streets' proposals are not born out of any concern for ordinary people or a love for the architecture of previous eras, but they are basically the latest phase in a half-century battle to erase the traces of the post-war years of social democracy. Council housing has been demonised, sold off, its construction has been prohibited, and Create Streets are part of a movement to erase its existence completely.

The demolition and rebuilding of estates would only ever make sense if the communities that are housed there were able to return to the new development with the same tenure arrangements as before, and of course, this is exactly what Create Streets advocate. But by the stage of the Savills report, the prospect of "decanting", meaning the eviction of the existing community, is explicitly ignored. And in practice, the last decades in the UK have seen all manner of examples of council estates being demolished with the promise of new homes for the community, only to see the residents dispersed after all.

In the case of Mount Pleasant, car parks have no existing community, so Create Streets no doubt saw this as a way to further their cause without exposing themselves to the issues on which they are actually vulnerable. But they couldn't help but employ the wincingly conservative architect Francis Terry, of the Terry dynasty, who have been crusading against the socialist horrors of modernism since Francis' father Quinlan left the Architectural Association in the late 1960s. The younger Terry designed a scheme ostensibly traditional, based on avenues and circuses, but sadly reminiscent of the pseudo-classical rubbish by American architects that made up the earliest stages of the Canary Wharf development in the late 1980s.

It seems extremely unlikely that the Mount Pleasant Association's attempt to change the course of development in the area will have much impact on what eventually gets built. At the end of the day, despite Create Streets' attempt to ground their sleight of hand by referring to the inalienable aesthetic will of the people, contemporary buildings have been selling perfectly well in London, indeed all too well. Bickering over whether the windows have fake sashes or not is completely beside the point, and the bottom line will decide in the end.

Once the first counterproposal for Mount Pleasant had appeared however, others sought to get involved, which is not surprising considering the proximity of the site to so many architects' offices. Thomas Heatherwick slated the original plans, and rumours appeared that he might make a proposal himself. Zaha Hadid, whose office sits just a few streets down the mail centre, also publicly mulled over whether to put together a proposal, although nothing of this came to light. But another local architect put together a scheme for the site that throws all the others into sharp relief.

Peter Barber runs a small office of around ten people in a shabby street near Kings Cross, just down the road from the mail centre, but his work has gathered attention far beyond his resources. He is one of the last architects working primarily on housing in the state sector, who remains true to certain principles of humane modernist architecture, namely that the abstract qualities of contemporary construction techniques allow for the creation of richer living spaces than "traditional" forms. Barber is a specialist in low-rise high-density, an approach to modernist housing that rejects tall buildings and uses clever effects in plan and section to create light-filled housing with gardens and other perks, on tight or difficult sites. His approach, which is consistent over a wide variety of different buildings, often uses cuts and clefts in buildings to create private outdoor areas, allowing for a wide range of spaces within tightly packed and often low-budget developments.

While the political arguments were raging over the different schemes for the Mount Pleasant site, Barber took the opportunity to design his own, which he called Coldbath Town.[51] Unlike the Royal Mail scheme, with its brick-clad blocks of speculation, or the Create Streets attempt to recreate Georgian utopia, Barber suggested a long ribbon of five-to-six-storey housing to follow the edge of the site, situated above an arcade in which shops and businesses would be located. Within this perimeter wall, the interior of the site would be made up of densely packed houses of two to three storeys, with qualities a little like those of a North African casbah.

Barber's scheme suggested an architecture that was full of ideas drawn from tradition, but also capable of adding to or manipulating historic material in the service of improving the performance of the dwellings themselves. But furthermore, it represented an architecture of housing that is not commodified, that is produced primarily for need rather than profit. Barber ends his description of the project with the suggestion that it be publicly funded, which is perhaps the most radical part of the whole idea.

The scheme, and a large plaster model of the houses encrusting the landscape, were exhibited at the Royal Academy's summer show 2015, at which they won the main architecture prize. There is no real future for it, although Barber has a wide number of projects at various stages of the construction process. But it demonstrates a vitally different attitude to that of the development industry, and of course that of Johnson. Nearly all the different schemes that Johnson "called in" during his mayorship were granted because he had made commitments to make a dent in the housing shortage, and any new houses were, as far as he was concerned, all to the good. In this sense it chimes with his desire to be always seen to be doing something, anything really, as long as something is being done.

It's perhaps too much to ask that Johnson behave any differently with regard to housing, considering his natural affinity with the sort of people who make up the development industry, and his inability to take any real serious risks that don't immediately benefit him. But a better Mayor would have taken planning seriously, as more than just a rubber-stamping tool, in fact one capable of helping to shape spaces and communities for the benefit of more than just the shareholders of the developers and pension funds who pay for the towers to be built.

#

One of the stranger things in Johnson's housing manifesto of 2008 was a declaration of interest in matters not just of provision, procurement, and delivery, but of design:

> Affordable housing must be more than 'decent'; it must be desirable. I will encourage developers to work with housing associations at the design stage to **improve the aesthetic quality of new developments**.[52]

This might sound a little bit like the arguments made by those like Create Streets to advocate the destruction of council estates, but the sentiment behind it has led to one of the strangest of the effects that Johnson has had upon the face of London, and beyond. If his immediate influence on the landscape of London was a series of vulgar and unnecessary structures, and one aspect of his tenure was a constant stream of large but unremarkable tall buildings, Johnson's inadvertent influence on the form of housing has been sobering, perhaps even a general improvement.

The team around Johnson prepared what was called the Mayor's London Housing Design Guide, a set of instructions and guidelines for the creation of new housing that were, in effect, the first set of space standards for new housing that had come along in a long time in the UK. In the past, the Parker Morris Report of 1961 had defined a set of standards for new housing that were intended to stipulate the minimum requirements of modern lifestyles. These included not just the overall size of dwellings based on the number of inhabitants, and not just the size of bedrooms and kitchens and so on, but also standards for amounts of storage and other spaces. The standards were widely adopted, and became a basic benchmark for the provision of housing in the UK. Almost all the council housing from that era was built to Parker Morris standards, which led on the one hand to a basic minimum across the country, but also challenged more ambitious designers to work on ways in which the space should be used to its best advantage through open-plan layouts, sliding partitions and other space-saving tricks.

In 1980, the new Conservative government abolished the housing standards, around the same time that councils were finally prevented from developing new housing through changes in law based on borrowing. What this meant was that the size of new housing, which in this period was primarily suburban, was allowed to follow what the market dictated, which meant, of course, smaller. Deregulation where many countries elsewhere in Europe maintained their minimum space standards meant that by the early years of the 21st century it was well known that the UK built the smallest new homes of any in Europe.

It was into this context that the Mayor's London Housing Design Guide[53] was published in August 2010, after a draft report in 2009 and a consultation period. Its most prominent feature was the introduction of a new set of minimum space standards, similar to but generally larger than the Parker Morris standards, in keeping with the more developed consumer economy of the 21st century. Initially these standards were only to apply to publicly funded housing, but they were rolled out to apply to all new developments seeking planning permission in London. For pushing forward with this new framework, if anything, Johnson should be credited.

But it wasn't just a new set of space standards that Johnson's design guide brought in. It also signalled a great change in the physical appearance of many of the new housing developments in London. The first pages of the London Housing Design Guide introduced a term that would come to signify much of what would be coming over the next few years: "A New London Vernacular". What this signified was the arrival of "austerity" thinking into the production of residential space in the capital. In the years after 1997, with all the confidence of the New Labour government, the residential construction market in London began to accelerate again. This was the point where Lord Rogers of Riverside was at his most influential, with his Cities for a Small Planet, and his leading the Urban Task Force. High-density development was in, and an architectural design methodology that utilised contemporary models of construction and a resurrected modernist aesthetic after the years of postmodern anti-urban design.

The neo-modernism of the Blair years was marked by a studious avoidance of the old council-house concrete look. New developments were often notable for their lightweight and brightly coloured cladding schemes, which were both cheap but also considered colourful enough that they didn't evoke memories of older modernist housing. The new developments were also high-density, marking a return to high-rise after generations of its rejection. This architecture became caustically referred to as "yuppiedromes", after their perceived role in the social cleansing of old housing estates and working-class areas by new money.

At the lowest ebb, the massive development of St George's Wharf in Vauxhall, which was designed by global archi-giant Broadway Malyan and whose first major phase was complete by 2006, has to be considered as one of the absolute worst developments of that whole era, an ugly, pointless mess, scattered with ridiculous gewgaws and extraneous structures, bulky, wanton, and offensive, an architectural insult only added to by the construction of a mammoth tower right next to it a decade later.

Other designs of the era were less nakedly aggressive, but even well-respected firms like AHMM could, by the time of the financial crash, be widely parodied for their wacky cladding, their little multicoloured balconies, their occasionally trite references to long-lost industry that once occupied the site before either decline or regeneration had done their work.

It was this context for architecture that the design guide referred to when it stated that "In general, London's housing should not be striving for 'iconic' architecture" — utilising the word which had by that point become a pejorative for abject flashiness — "but should focus on great background architecture made of durable materials that weather well." The aim, such as it was, was to turn away from individualistic blocks that yelled out their own narcissism, and instead to utilise planning guidelines to encourage developers to create new housing that was not just about making money, but also about making new, integrated bits of city.

Only two years later, a document published by Urban Design London proclaimed that, indeed, a "New London Housing Vernacular" had been created. Within only a short period, various elements of the design guide had created a sea change in development, which was obvious to anyone moving around the capital. A few specific elements of the guide were touted as being particularly important, such as the expressed demand for large numbers of ground-level entrances rather than lifts and corridor access, as well as reducing the numbers of individual housing units that would be accessed from each entrance. This meant that architects and clients were encouraged to utilise terrace and tenement forms that are more familiar from London history than modern apartment types, adding a certain urban consistency to the process.

Another aspect of the design guide was the encouragement of more "tenure blindness" in developments, meaning that the difference between private, affordable, and social rented apartments would not be quite as apparent as it often turned out, with some developments giving entirely different entrance facilities for different tenures, a phenomenon known as "poor doors". Again, terraced housing with multiple entrances provided an existing methodology that was able to accommodate this kind of thinking.

But there was much going on in the new housing developments under discussion that was coming directly from the designers — such as the use of predominantly vertically proportioned windows, or the deliberate separation of the building into an obvious base-middle-top tripartite structure. Both of these are what you would find in buildings of previous centuries, and while a lot of the new housing architecture was in no way historic in terms of its detailing or decoration, the architects were still drawing on the Georgian and Victorian precedents for these spatial cues.

But the most obvious development in this New London Housing Vernacular was the sudden comprehensive return of bricks. If you were a British builder 150 years ago, the way you would build a house would be to build large solid walls of brick, a decorated front and plainer back, and party walls between houses that incorporated chimney flues. The roof would be timber, as would the internal floors, and of course the window frames and doors. This kind of construction is heavy on the outside, with the internals of the building far lighter. Above a certain size, this isn't how things are built now. These days, nearly any building has a concrete core containing lifts and stairs, and a steel or concrete frame including the floors. This is the basic rigid skeleton, and nowadays the exterior of the building is relatively light, and attached to the frame as cladding.

But in the context of the New London Housing Vernacular, these modern buildings were suddenly being covered in bricks, not laid by workmen on site with spirit levels and cement, but assembled offsite into panels, which were then lifted into place and clipped back onto the frame. The constructional methodology is entirely false, the appearance of crafted labour is synthetic, the bricks are quite often only skin-deep, but the effect is to tie these new developments into the historic London streetscape in a far more apparently integrated way than was normal. A new housing development — such as the permitted scheme for Mount Pleasant — could consist of many multi-storey concrete buildings, all of which would be clad in various different kinds of brick, as if they were just extra-large examples of all the terraces that make up so much of London.

There are a number of reasons for why this happened so suddenly. The first is of course the design guide, which called specifically for new housing to engage more meaningfully with the existing London context. This meant that developers could see that there was a basically low-risk route through the planning process, where new buildings could be described as taking their place within an existing urban context rather than trying to overcome it. The upshot of this is that the new developments are apparently more "in keeping" with what was there before, which makes them less likely to be controversial, at least in terms of superficial aesthetics.

But another factor is generational. The architects who largely ran the firms designing the housing of the early 2000s were often those that had matured in a British context dominated by Lords Foster and Rogers. They had struggled to make good work when postmodernism was at its height, and when the mood shifted they wanted to design in a modern way again, without making what were considered the mistakes of the 1960s. But the architects who were pushing some of the earliest and best examples of this new vernacular architecture were often younger (in their forties), and had a different attitude to design, being concerned with what are perhaps more continental attitudes to history, where new architecture is capable of re-interpreting an existing condition without lessening its originality. Firms such as Maccreanor Lavington or Karakusevic Carson were some of the earliest adopters of this new austerity architecture.

It must be stressed that this development has been to a large extent a good thing — buildings designed according to these ideas are generally better architecture than those that made up the bulk of the pre-crash production, and Johnson does deserve credit for helping to raise the standard in this way. But as with any good idea in architecture, it is easily ruined. The first problem is perhaps superficial, but has to do with herd mentality. Since this architecture first appeared, it has become extremely popular with clients, to the point of pathetic ubiquity. Now we see brick-clad towers of nearly thirty storeys (the tallest load-bearing brick walls in the world, on the Monadnock Building in Chicago, are seventeen) being constructed, we see old office blocks beings converted into flats and in the process having their glass skins taken off and replaced with brick, we see any old nonsense being clad in dingy brown brick in the hope that it will be given an easy time through planning.

Particularly egregious examples I've seen include a new house added to the end of a terrace of modernist houses from the 1960s that were built by Camden Council at a time they were producing avant-garde council housing of an extremely high quality. The new building is respectful of the *form* of what's there, but in the current climate couldn't possibly respect the material choice, and so completes the terrace of white-painted concrete houses incongruously in brick, in one of the only places it isn't actually in keeping. I've even seen London-style neo-vernacular buildings going up in other cities that have no real brick tradition, so knee-jerk and uninspired has the approach become. In fact, in 2015 a Europe-wide brick shortage was reported, with lead-in times of years, after so many London projects became skinned that way.

The other problem is that no amount of skin-deep context can hide the fact that most of these buildings are still just as obviously socially awful financial investment items as their shinier cousins. Brick-clad housing blocks are often praised for their contextual consciousness, even when they sit on the site of demolished council homes, the new buildings completely out of the reach of any but the richest residents. In a city that has been undergoing so much housing struggle, no amount of tasteful brick detailing can mask the problems.

"They are no happier than anyone else; they just have more money"

The Rich in Johnson's London

If one of the defining characteristics of the housing market of the early 2000s was the appearance of "yuppiedromes" — the new wave of unaffordable private apartments and the aspirational "regeneration" lifestyle branding that accompanied them — then the post-crash landscape of London pushed this to ridiculous lengths. The struggles of making rent and getting by were conducted to a backdrop of ever-more-offensive property advertising, ascending to a level of offensive pretentiousness that hit its apex with a 2015 film released by developers Redrow for a development they called The London Collection. In fact this was until recently a concrete skeleton above Aldgate Underground Station that for half a decade had stood unfinished, wrapped in scaffolding, waiting for someone to raise the money to complete it.

The innocent enough mistake that the makers of Redrow made was to try something a little bit different; in this case a short film that showed a thirty-ish white man in a City-ish suit struggling through crowds of pedestrians, working late, looking stressed, passionately kissing a woman in a lift, all the while dramatically recounting gobbets of motivational chat about struggling to the top in order to look down on the city from his penthouse and say "I did this". It was typically narcissistic nonsense of course, but its pitch-perfect sociopathy and disdain for city life itself, in favour of the solipsistic penthouse view of shimmering towers and lights, meant that it became almost instantly infamous, and was quickly withdrawn in a shower of newspaper opinion columns.

But this was only one of hundreds of tasteless examples of property marketing over the Johnson years, from developments in largely Caribbean areas being depicted entirely occupied by white people, to hideously decorated "hipster" models with foot-long moustaches adorning the billboards on the site of what had been council housing only a few months before, to the endlessly crass naming conventions of new developments: Atlas, Mettle & Poise, Aykon, Vibe, Artisan, etc., and all the incredibly vulgar taglines that go along with them.

The strange thing is that largely these messages aren't really meant for the people walking past them. Because if anything, the property market over the Johnson years became even more abstract, even more alienated, as the yuppiedrome concept became supplanted by the fear of the influence of the overseas investor, buying property in London without ever planning to set foot in the area, continually inflating the cost of property and threatening to tear the social fabric of the city apart once and for all. This fear not only speaks of the truth of London's global status and condition, but it also acts as a sign of the resentment and fear that, in parts of the UK not blessed by the dazzling wealth of the Southeast, helped to later fuel the "Brexit" vote.

It's true that the relative influence of foreign money over both the development and distribution of property has been a major source of social concern over the last decade. The peculiar character of world politics over the period 2008–16 has brought a number of different characters into public consciousness, always skating on the thin ice of xenophobia. The influences could be repulsive, whether it was a fear of kleptocracy in the post-Soviet world, the earth-shaking events of the Arab Spring or the effects of the Eurozone crisis on the southern countries, but they could also be attractive, as new wealthy constituencies in various parts of the developing world found themselves able to invest in the rich economies for the first time. But the sense of the growing influence of the ultra-rich has been tangible.

One of the favourite characters for Londoners is the Russian oligarch, some of whom own the most expensive properties in the capital, and who have occasionally been known to get involved in their murky businesses in London. A long-running saga concerned the presence of Boris Berezovsky and his entourage of anti-Putin dissidents, leading to the murder by radioactive poison of Alex Litvinenko in 2006, a scandal that rumbled on throughout the years of Johnson's tenure, up to and beyond the eventual suicide of Berezovsky in 2013.

The ultra-rich of the Gulf have been characters on the London scene since the oil boom after WWII, when they made inroads into Mayfair and other parts of London, ruffling the feathers of the established elite. They are still to be found in their favourite parts of London, making headlines when they fly over their fleets of gold-plated supercars and other such deliriously unsubtle displays of wealth.

But the newest players on the global property scene have been the investors from the new wealthy of the Far East, from the Singaporean middle classes making small profits from buying and selling on houses long before they are even constructed, to the growing class of ultra-wealthy Chinese, making the most of capitalism with Chinese characteristics. The particular character of state involvement in their economy has meant that deals with individual Chinese businessmen are often proxy deals with the Chinese state, with the two working hand in hand on foreign investments.

There are a number of different ways that global investors are involved in the London property market. At the top are the ultra-rich like Lakshmi Mittal, the billionaires who spend many millions on their properties, buying up whole swathes of Mayfair or all the penthouse apartments in towers, or in one particular Russian's case, the largest residence in London that isn't itself Buckingham Palace. Commentators cry about the unlit windows, the strangling of life as more and more housing goes into the ownership of people who spend only a few weeks a year in the house, if that.[54]

But it's not just the ultra-rich. The mega-rich, those who work in the top jobs in finance, have seen their fortunes not only maintained but thoroughly improved. The power of the City and its ability to dispense vast salaries has fed the property boom, contributing to such phenomena as the proliferation of "mega-basements", the residential towers that sprout up in the poor neighbourhoods bounding the City or Canary Wharf, not to mention the boom in restaurant and leisure uses in Central London.

How did Johnson deal with this kind of situation? He had made overtures to dealing with the housing crisis when the new coalition government embarked on the austerity drive, but a few years further down the line, in November 2013, when the anti-austerity resistance had shown itself toothless and inadequate, Johnson felt safe enough to write one of his "chicken feed" *Telegraph* columns on the subject of the ultra-rich, and how they were being blamed for so much.

"We should be humbly thanking the super-rich, not bashing them",[55] said the headline. Johnson took his trouble to identify the super-rich as a strange minority akin to "Irish travellers" and "ex-gang members", and expressed an admiration for them as a distinct sub-culture of which he most definitely was not lucky enough to be a part, despite all the background evidence to the contrary. Johnson's argument, such as it was, was that the super-rich were "Tax Heroes", with the top one percent of society contributing nearly thirty percent of all tax revenues. He contrasted this against the late 1970s, when income tax was much higher before Thatcherism, when the one percent contributed only eleven percent. In a fantastically disingenuous sleight of hand, Johnson took this as a good thing — suggesting that lower taxes meant that higher earners contributed more, rather than the fact that back then the one percent of top earners actually earned a much smaller amount of the total wages in society.

The context for all this was the "banker bashing" that was going on in Britain at this point, as campaigns to highlight tax avoidance and rapidly widening inequality were prominent in the media. Johnson may have posed as a disinterested observer, but in columns like this, he was representing his own people, those from whom he came, those who put him where he was, and those that he would most rely on for his future ambitions. In the end, it's about little more than class.

\#

Johnson's paeans to the elite are a far cry from his occasional forays into everyman rhetoric, but they are part of the general attitude of the man, where nothing is to be taken quite seriously, when a certain consistency of charm and laxness lubricate the journey through politics. It's the sort of thing that politicians pick up through the years of learning the media and working with PR teams and spin doctors, but with a twist: instead of relentlessly hammering a strictly set-up message, a more old-fashioned public-school way of conversational speech — convincing enough, confident, but clearly lacking in sincerity — is the method of conversing with the public.

In October 2010, Johnson made headlines when he said that "we will not accept any kind of Kosovo-style social cleansing of London".[56] But his strangely clumsy phrasing, perhaps delivered as part of an exchange of warning shots with the new Prime Minister David Cameron, belies what happened throughout London during his tenure. Johnson's faults on this front are basically down to his pandering to his natural constituencies, his laziness and his unwillingness to get involved in a struggle with no direct benefit to him. But in doing so, he has been aided and abetted by incompetents from all over the political spectrum, including a number of Labour-led councils who have behaved disgracefully when it has come to regeneration and property.

The question of whether the social cleansing that has occurred in London over the last decade is "Kosovo-style" is irrelevant. What has been undoubtedly happening is some form of peripheralisation, although its full extents are hard to map. There is anecdotal evidence, for example the eastward drift of the locations that young families of certain social classes and professions have been forced to look for houses to buy, from Hackney to Homerton, then across the Lea Valley to Stratford, Leyton, and Walthamstow, traditionally poor areas, in some ways more suburban in character than some inner-city area newly discovered by the young bourgeoisie.

But beyond anecdotes of the relatively privileged, there have been many cases of distant dispersal. Over Johnson's term the news was often filled with stories about families being "decanted" from their council homes in order to demolish and rebuild, with the council then offering them properties in towns down the Kent coast, or as far away as towns in the north of England. The waiting lists for housing are so long, and the budget cuts and restrictions on local government are so strict, that these long-range dispersals appear to make sense to the authorities enacting them.

In one example from 2013, a group of young mothers who had been living at a hostel in Stratford were told by the local council, Newham, that the centre was being closed. Some of the women were offered temporary accommodation in places as distant as Manchester, while others were threatened with homelessness. But rather than just accept the destruction of their social and community relationships through a forced relocation, twenty-nine of these families gathered together and took matters into their own hands, starting a campaign, not only to help themselves, but to draw attention to a terrible situation.

The Focus E15 Mothers took their campaign to the streets. At one side of the Olympic Park is the Carpenter's Estate, a network of low-rise houses and three high-rise blocks dating from the 1970s. These blocks were once the highest and boldest structures in the area, but in the gold rush around the Olympic Park they have become dwarfed by a selection of crass apartment towers in various different shiny shades of cheap metal cladding. Over the last decade various different plans have been

The Carpenter's Estate - Once looming tower blocks now amongst the smaller objects in the Stratford landscape. (Image author's own).

put forward for demolishing the estate, with University College London at one point planning to build a new campus on the site as part of the Olympic "legacy". Despite campaigns by the residents, the estate has been progressively decanted, with it now standing mostly empty, looking out at the Orbit, whose twists poke out over the barbed wire that guards the dilapidated old light-industrial buildings still sitting beside the railways.

The Focus E15 mothers took over a number of empty buildings on the estate, turning them into a community centre, and with the help of housing activists, they got their message out — that communities were being destroyed, that the housing crisis was causing genuine and real suffering to vulnerable people. They protested evictions, led protests outside the property fair MIPIM, an event for which was occurring at the Excel Centre down by the docks, and they created a petition that got given to Johnson with thousands of signatories on it. Their campaign received a lot of coverage in the media, and they won some tactical victories, such as removing the threat of their being moved from London, but of course the struggle goes on.

To the south of the river, another housing scandal showed the human costs both of Johnson's disinterest, and also of the complacency of Labour councils. The Heygate Estate was built in the early 1970s near to the Elephant and Castle roundabout, a working-class neighbourhood in Southwark, famous for its traffic roundabout and dilapidated shopping centre. The Heygate was a system-built estate, made almost entirely of prefabricated concrete panels, during the largely discredited flirtation between the British construction industry and factory production-line technology. The estate was made of a number of low-rise blocks around courtyards, surrounded by four tall and imposing long slab blocks, and the whole estate was linked by a network of raised walkways, separating cars and pedestrians.

On the one hand, the uncompromising concrete architecture combined with a bad reputation meant that the Heygate had become one of the main London examples of a "concrete jungle", used as a filming location for a wide range of films, adverts, and music videos, usually with a dystopian flavour. But by the early 2000s its landscape had matured, with so many large trees that it appeared a little like a group of pavilions nestled within a forest.

But over the early 2000s the estate was marked for demolition, with the Australian property developer Lend Lease negotiating with Southwark Council to take over the land and build new housing. Despite evidence that the buildings were sound and could be refurbished, and despite the promises of the residents that they liked their estate, and despite the fact that it had a low crime rate for the area, the decision was taken to compulsorily purchase the land, demolish the 1,200 dwellings on the site, in order to transform it into Elephant Park, a new development of nearly 3,000 dwellings.

The Heygate saga was only one of the most celebrated of the housing disasters of the last decade, and nearly all of it happened under Johnson's tenure. The residents were originally told they would have new houses on the estate, and then were told not. Those who had bought their houses were compensated at prices well below what the estimated prices of even the smallest unit on the new development would be. The number of social rented flats in the new development was negotiated down from hundreds to just seventy-nine. The deal that Lend Lease negotiated with Southwark Council for the land was revealed to be worth just £50 million, after the council had already spent way more than that amount on moving the residents out and demolishing the existing buildings.

Maps prepared around this time by the campaign group Heygate Was Home showed the dispersal of those who had lived in the Heygate, both those who were council tenants, rehoused by the council, and also those who had been leaseholders, who had bought their houses, and who had to move wherever their money could actually take them. The basic fact shown by these maps was an explosive dispersal from their location in what despite its long-lasting poverty was a prime spot in Central London, and thus the homogenisation of the inner-city community as a result.

The Heygate saga was a depressing and prominent case, and when it came down to giving his approval to the masterplan, Johnson's quote was telling: "It is vital that we push forward with work to unlock the massive economic potential of the Elephant & Castle area which has languished in a no-man's land for too many years."[57] Out of context, perhaps, but it speaks volumes about the social situation that entire communities could be said to have been living on "no-man's land" for nearly forty years. By this point in his mayoral career it was clear there was no revolt coming, and Johnson could refer to type. Economic activity was good, an increase in homes was good, and it didn't really matter what type of homes. Johnson just needed to look after his kind of people.

\#

In the years after the crash I found myself at one point working for an architect, one of whose specialties was workplaces, both in terms of their design but also analysis and evaluation. A project that I didn't work on but that I witnessed involved a very strange sort of consultancy. An anonymous client, working through an agency, was thinking of investing in a new office building in London. At that point, roughly 2010, there were a number of stumps sitting in the City, empty sites that had been demolished but upon which construction had given up after 2008. Many of these sites had planning permission for towers of upwards of two hundred metres in height, huge office blocks from a previous boom, already with their silly little nicknames in place — the Cheesegrater, the Walkie Talkie, the Pinnacle, etc.

The client wanted to know if it was worth their while investing in one of these unbuilt projects, and were feeling especially cautious, and in no mood to waste any money. They wanted to know how good the office space inside the buildings was, and how much they might be able to rent them out for. The architects were tasked with analysing the planning permissions, looking at size, servicing, efficiency, views, and other factors, to help the client decide.

What was telling was how this study went — the first building rejected was the Pinnacle, which, when unveiled by American architects KPF, was an example of highly advanced digital design, with cladding panels that varied in form across the whole facade, and a form that from a distance appeared something like a helter-skelter or spiral. The problem was that this slender visual quality translated into a rather ungainly rounded plan form, almost like a sliced brain, which completely lacked the efficiency required. This was rejected, and it was interesting that this was one of the only large towers that didn't end up being picked up when the construction industry got swinging again.

Another still-unbuilt building was more of interest to this client, however. It had large square-ish floor plates, with a centrally located core, which potentially gave much better value for money. Even better, the floors towards the top of the building were larger than those to the bottom, meaning that there was more area available at the points in the building where the rent would be highest. The deal was back on.

20 Fenchurch Street - Looming overhead, swelling outwards, pictured before it began melting the luxury cars of London. (Image author's own)

A few years later the building — the aforementioned "Walkie Talkie", 20 Fenchurch Street — was built, and was about to hit the news for what was a most incredible reason, one whose heavy-handed satirical resonance was hard to miss. In late summer 2013, as it neared completion, it was reported that the concave curved south facade of the building was focusing the sun's rays onto the streets below, causing melting damage to a businessman's parked Jaguar car.[58] The embarrassed client quickly asked for permission to install sunshades on the facade, which sit there to this day, and the transformation of a brand new skyscraper into a comedy Bond villain's weapon trained on the public below was all too indicative of this period of development.

But the "Walkie Talkie", the "Shard", the "Cheesegrater", and many of these new skyscrapers may have been built while Johnson was Mayor, but their conception, design, and planning process were all completed in the years before the crash, under the eye of Ken Livingstone and the then-head of City of London planning department Peter Rees. The decision to encourage tall buildings in the City was part of Livingstone's Faustian pact, whereby finance and development were to be encouraged as long as taxes were paid and some form of redistribution might occur.

Rees, who was in his role for thirty years until 2015, and had overseen more than one construction boom, developed the idea in the 2000s that there was an appropriate point in the City of London that would be suitable for a "cluster" of tall buildings, mainly down Leadenhall, where there were already one or two tall buildings and a collection of middle-aged office blocks that it would be politically easy to demolish. From this thinking came first the "Gherkin", the exceptionally phallic office tower designed by Foster and Partners that gave rise to the whole silly naming game.

As he made his approach towards City Hall, Johnson sensed that there was political capital to be made out of a general sense that London was developing too rapidly, and he made much of protecting views of historic buildings, claiming that "I believe well-designed tall buildings should play a part in London's development, but they must not overshadow existing landmarks". This was basically a dig at Livingstone, whose London Plan at that point made it clear that tall buildings were to be promoted. And of course, as a Tory, it was expected of Johnson that he would play the heritage card at this point.

The term that came to stick to Johnson on this front was "Dubai-on-Thames", a riff on Henley-on-Thames, where Johnson had been MP in the years leading up to his mayoral bid. The expectation was that, what with his rightward leanings, his rejection of Livingstone, not to mention the financial crisis, the skyline of London would be safe enough. But sure enough, partly through the general and immense pressure that operates at that level, but of course partly due to laziness and a love of money, there wasn't much that Johnson was willing to do to stand in the way of development.

And while the crash did put an end to various proposed towers, in the years since the vertical pressure has been building back up. Most of the sites that were lying empty in the city have been filled, and there's another batch passing through planning, less "iconic" in form than before, more concerned with maximising rentable space. Outside of the City, similar things have been occurring, with various "clusters" of high buildings being proposed, including along stretches of the Thames that had been languishing as non-residential areas of light industry right up until a few years ago. This level of actual and proposed activity raised a level of panic, with the *Architects Journal* and the *Observer* setting up The Skyline Campaign in early 2014 to raise awareness of the more than two hundred different towers of over two hundred metres in height that were currently in construction or had planning permission.

But "Dubai-on-Thames" is pushing it. Most of London's towers would fit more in a mid-western American City than a hypertrophic petro-settlement like in the Emirates. 308 metres, the height of the Shard, isn't even the tallest building in Europe any more. So on the one hand, who could genuinely hold back the demand for this kind of space, in a financial landscape fuelled by quantitative easing, massive inward investment from abroad, and a runaway wealthy class? But it's the endless "yes yes yes" that is galling, that there are institutions and talents that would be able to channel this kind of energy into urban relationships that were not almost entirely dictated by the fashions of speculation. But it seems that even a little bit of planning is a utopian idea at this point.

#

Unfortunately, it would be naive to argue that the only problem with the development of London over the Johnson years was a lack of positive planning for public spaces and other goods. Unfortunately, if you let money people have carte blanche, there is a tendency for everything to become fetid and dank. Call it the innate corruptibility of human beings, or simply the fact that it's easier to deal and work with people you know and might owe favours to, but the stench of cronyism and dodgy favours hung around the Johnson administration. This was both in terms of his hiring and firing of friends and helpers, but also the procurement of large projects, including, alongside the vanity ones, the reconstruction of large parts of the city.

In May 2013 it was announced that a kilometre-long strip of empty land along the northern edge of the Royal Albert Dock in Newham was to finally be redeveloped, after languishing for decades following the conclusion of

Royal Albert Docks - Post-industrial emptiness awaiting transformation into pan-global trade zone. (Image author's own).

upstream docking on the Thames. The Royal Albert was opened in 1880, and alongside the Royal Victoria (1855) and the King George V (1925) docks it made up the Royal Docks, which were once the largest group of enclosed docks in the world. The north side of the Royal Albert had sat empty for many years, cleared of its warehouses and cranes, facing the airport runway directly to its south.

At one end to the east, the University of East London had built a campus in the late 1990s, with buildings designed by Ted Cullinan Architects, a decent enough quality but dispiritingly Blairite neo-modern architecture, all drums and prow-like shapes in different colours. At the west end of the dock is Newham Dockside, a thoroughly basic commercial building that was completed in 2004, sat empty for three years and was finally taken over by Newham council in 2007, serving as their headquarters ever since. To the north, over a wide but never busy road, is Beckton, a working-class neighbourhood once dominated by the huge gas works, but now languishing — like so many other places — in post-industrial uncertainty.

Newham Council received a great deal of press over the Johnson years as one of the front lines of the housing crisis. Whether it was their attempts to move tenants out of London to places as far away as Stoke, resulting in the campaign of the Focus E15 Mothers, or whether it was the scandal of "beds-in-sheds" and overcrowding, both of which were focussed on Newham, the plight of the poor of East London during the housing crises was perhaps most acutely visible here. The Labour-controlled council were to a certain extent trapped — by spending cuts on the one hand and the housing shortage on another —

and it is true that they have made efforts to tackle rogue landlords. But theirs is a story of a local authority many of whose residents are in acute need, who lack the funds to do very much at all beyond providing basic services.

But this is still only part of the story. Because if the downward financial pressure was largely the result of the decisions of central government to use the financial crisis as an opportunity to continue the harrying of local government that had been going on since the 1980s, then the ways around it had to come from somewhere. Newham may have protested heavily regarding their troubles, but certain of their actions didn't exactly do them any credit.

In 2014 a video came to the attention of the British Press that Newham Council had prepared for a display they had at the 2010 Shanghai Expo, the first major world exposition in a long time, and along with the Beijing Olympics, one of the most significant diplomatic events held as part of the Chinese boom. The video, subtitled in Mandarin, was clearly aimed at the home audience, and was essentially a sales pitch for Newham, looking to see if there was investment that could be attracted.

The video's title was "Regeneration Supernova", and represents a prime example of the corporate end of the promotional video genre of which the Redrow "American Psycho" video was the more domestic end. "London is moving East", it said, as an animated satellite view zoomed in from near-earth orbit to Newham, in a strange inversion of the classic Eastenders opening sequence. Apparently, so said the video, there was an "Arc of Opportunity" that stretched from the Olympics in the north, down the Lea, and then swooping around to the Royal Docks.

Commentators at the time[59] noted the clear and crass offering-up of large parts of the city for private sale to global investors, but latched onto the sheer extremity of the erasure that was implied. Newham here was renamed "Newham London", the old estate agent's trick of upping the attractiveness of an area through sneaky nomenclature, and like any property investment "offer" it was shown as virgin land defined only by its connections to transport hubs and ways of connecting to other parts of the world. The "Arc of Opportunity" conveniently swept alongside most of the parts of Newham where people actually live, an ignorance of existing communities that was summed up by the title of the whole thing — a supernova may be bright, but it is of course the last burst of a dying star.

Sure enough, the client who had been enticed along to invest in the windswept waterfront of Newham was the suitably enigmatically titled Advanced Business Park, a Chinese development company led by Xu Weiping, whose CV was also rather blurry in detail. Their intention was to invest more than £1 billion into transforming the zone into the Asian Business Port (ABP), a development of almost five million square feet of office space for Chinese companies looking to set up regional headquarters in the UK.

The proposals that were published showed a basically planned grid of buildings, all mid-rise, all office blocks. It was a perfectly blank example of global business park architecture, well-connected zones severed from their territories, defined more by airports, broadband and business standards than by any urban relationships themselves. In this it's more symptomatic of the character of a "global city" than almost any of the other projects in this book, an anonymous business park that quite literally might as well be on the outskirts of Shanghai, Abu Dhabi, Bangalore, Santiago, Dallas, Lagos, or anywhere.

The ABP proposals were met with a little dismay, even in more conservative circles, and Johnson sought to allay fears of a general sell-off of the UK, saying, whilst on a trade mission to China,

> It would be economic folly for us somehow to say we're going to cut ourselves off from external investment and external interest [...] That has never been a sensible way for a country to conduct itself. It would deprive us of absolutely vital sources of finance and mean we're unable to go ahead with thousands and thousands of homes that our country needs.[60]

Not everything was quite as smooth as all that, however. The first shake-up came after investigations into Advanced Business Park.[61] The company, and Xu Weiping, were a bit of a mystery, with just one large development outside Beijing already completed. It was basically assumed that the operation was just yet another arm of the Chinese state, a semi-capitalist enterprise with a completely opaque structure. But it was soon discovered that the company had been sharing an office in Beijing with a company called London & Partners, an agency that had been set up by City Hall to attract inward investment to London. The problem with this was that L&P were part of the tendering process for the ABP project, apparently involved in judging the fitness of the Chinese bid. The accusation was that this was rather a cosy arrangement for a publicly funded body supposedly part of an impartial assessment.

A further objection to the project came through an investigation into the behaviour of the developer in their own work in China. It was alleged that they had engaged in human-rights abuses, including illegally demolishing homes to make way for development, and not compensating those they evicted. One might say that this is unlikely to have made them particularly unique in the context of the Chinese property boom, but the question of why this might not have been part of the tendering process was important.

But there was more again. There was one particular figure drifting around the outskirts of the ABP project who seemed to be slightly out of place. Xuelin Bates is a Chinese architect and property developer, who had an involvement in the early stages of the ABP project, apparently recommending the site to Xu Weiping, and registering a company to promote the project. The problem with this is that Bates was also a substantial donor to the Conservative Party, giving over £160,000 over a two-year period between 2010 and 2012. Again, there were considerable questions to be asked about the robustness of the procurement process.

It soon became clear, however, that Bates was also involved in another Johnsonian project, namely the ZhongRhong Group's attempt to build the Crystal Palace. She was listed as a sponsor of ZhongRhong's bid to take over the site, in documents provided as part of the negotiations with Bromley Council, and was known to have had meetings with the GLA and the London Development Agency, years prior to the initial announcement about the Palace project.[62]

Bates is also Lady Xuelin Bates, as she is married to the Conservative peer Lord Bates, making all the connections and donations seem rather circular. The implications of the secrecy and surreptitiousness of the connections led to the House of Lords Committee for Privileges and Conduct investigating Lord Bates' behaviour over the Crystal Palace rebuild, and in particular whether he should have registered an interest. The investigation cleared Lord Bates, although it did include the juicy detail that Ni Zhaoxing completely ignored the House of Lords' official requests for information.[63]

Of course, none of this information constitutes evidence of any kind of illegal activity. But what it speaks of is the kind of generalised corruption that seeps in when business interests are allowed to operate without scrutiny. In industries such as development that are so complex, politically significant, and involve huge sums of money, the tendency is for informal contacts to become an overwhelming structure. Why would you tender for every single job if you knew someone you'd worked with before who was perfectly capable? And why wouldn't you throw a bit of work to someone whose company had been such a strong supporter in the past?

The Johnson administration, time and time again, showed that once a deal had been agreed, the rules were only there as a guideline, and procedures had to be seen to be followed only for the sake of ticking boxes. But this has effects, whether it's the taxpayer who has to pick up the bill for a vanity project, or the communities moved aside for development, or the whole areas of the city rendered unliveable to anyone but the rich. It's a generalised move against the very idea that there may be a public realm, that everyone has a stake in a place. Johnson wanted us to feel sympathy for the ultra-rich because they paid a lot of tax, a courtesy he didn't exactly extend to the public in general, seeing as he only met them when they shouted at him in the street, rather than in a quiet corner of some global wealth jamboree.

"I have complete confidence in the police and I think that they are doing a very, very good job"

Disorder in Johnson's London

A large and not insignificant part of London's history relates to violence. For hundreds of years, there were neighbourhoods where it was not considered safe to go, such as Southwark in the time of Shakespeare, or the clusters of streets memorably rendered as "vicious, semi-criminal" on Booth's 19th-century poverty maps. Charles Dickens based much of his writing on the conditions of those trapped in what were called rookeries, the hyper-dense slums built up over generations, which were swept away in later waves of urban regeneration.

Sometimes this violence is related to specific and sporadic events, such as the Jack the Ripper killings, which still draw tourists to be guided round the alleyways of gentrified Spitalfields, or the legend of the Krays, the traces of whose exploits are still just about tangible in the atmosphere of one or two pubs in Bethnal Green and Mile End. At other times the sense of violence is more general, such as the destruction wrought by the Blitz, the memorable christening of Lower Clapton Road in Hackney as "Murder Mile" after a late-'90s spate of gun crime, or the fear of terrorism that for many years was associated with the Irish, and in more recent years Muslims. At other times as well the worries are related to the mob, whether it was Wat Tyler and the Peasant's Revolt in 1381, or the Battle of Cable Street in 1936, when locals battled police to prevent a British Union of Fascists march, or the Brixton Riots of 1981.

But there is a definite sense now in London that the city is safer than it was for a long time. Much like in New York, the decline that the city had suffered from the 1970s on had led to fears of "no-go" areas, severe drug epidemics that led to explosions of petty crime, and a sense of despondency. But in recent years, the city seems safer, there's more activity on the streets, cafe and restaurant culture has thrived where pubs have declined, and working-class neighbourhoods have had an influx of the middle classes, whose feeling that they might be about to get their head kicked in in large parts of the capital seems to have largely evaporated.

Of course, it's impossible to tell if this is actually the case. Crime statistics are rarely consistent in their collection year to year, so it's almost impossible to get a grasp on trends, while all manner of biases are known to affect how people perceive their own safety. But the sense of crime is a major political issue, and the old question of law-and-order can form a large part of the public perception of a politician.

And on this front, Johnson began as a bit of an unknown quantity. As a Tory politician he was supposed and expected to be an authoritarian, fond of imprisonment and vengeance against criminals, and lacking in sympathy. But for a Tory MP he had been rather to the enlightened side in terms of social issues, although little specifically to do with crime. On the one hand, he was from the more bohemian side of the upper classes, and of course in their topsy-turvy world sometimes Eton is seen as one of the more liberal schools; but on the other hand there was the Darius Guppy episode, where Johnson appeared willing to become an accessory to assault.

Johnson's manifesto in 2008 took a line more authoritarian than Livingstone, with pledges to add more community-support officers on the buses, after Livingstone's free bus travel for the young was seen to have resulted in a spike of crime on transport. Johnson also banned alcohol on public transport, for much the same reason. But the main pledge in the crime manifesto was that Johnson would take on the role of chair of the Metropolitan Police Association, something Livingstone had not done.

Throughout his years as Mayor, Johnson would be regularly tested on law-and-order issues, tests that he did not cope very well with. He was personally fortunate (all Londoners were fortunate) that he did not have to be seen to be in control after a major terror attack, as based upon other events it seems very unlikely that he would have been able to comport himself with the necessary gravitas. But many of these issues involved political unrest of different kinds, and Johnson's response to these left a lot to be desired.

The first major test of Johnson's management of law and order came when he'd been in place for just under a year. On 1st April 2009, a variety of demonstrations were called in Central London to protest the G20 summit that was taking place at the Excel Centre on Royal Victoria Docks. There was no real hope of anyone making it anywhere near the docks, so the Bank of England was the primary focus for protests. Four different groups, each led by a "horseman of the apocalypse", approached the bank from different directions, for an event called "G20 Meltdown", while a little further east an event called "Climate Camp" was taking place.

I attended the events that day, meeting a group of friends in the area, and drifting slowly through the shadowy streets of the City of London, at a little distance from the main event. The event was more carnivalistic than a march organised by a trade union might have been, and there appeared to be lots of small groups moving this way and that. At Bank there were speeches given, and yells of "JUMP!" could be heard directed at the bemused City workers looking down, while passing the Climate Camp we saw hundreds of people sitting in the middle of the road. Later in the afternoon we noted that there were more and more police arriving into the area, so we left and went to join others in the pub.

It was just as well we did, as the Metropolitan Police and their hardcore division the Territorial Support Group were getting ready to deploy what became one of the most infamous police tactics of recent times, the "kettle". Towards the late afternoon, hundreds of police, in two separate locations, formed a tight human barrier around the protests, preventing anyone from entering or leaving the area. These barriers were held until late evening, when protesters were gradually let out in slow streams to clear the area. Naturally, tempers fray in such a situation, and on the one hand protesters were accused of aggression towards the police, while the police were seen to be using their weapons against unarmed protestors, who at the climate camp were sitting on the ground calling out "this is not a riot!"

The next day, the media were filled with two significant stories. Nearly all the papers ran on their front page a photograph of a group of masked protesters staving in the windows of a branch of the Royal Bank of Scotland a street or two back from where the main protest was located. This is precisely the sort of picture the media want from an event like this, and of course it soon became apparent that the young people doing the smashing were at the time surrounded by a large number of photographers and cameramen desperate for just that sort of photo opportunity.

The other main story from the day was the news that a man had died in the protest. Forty-seven-year-old Ian Tomlinson was working as a street vendor for the *Evening Standard*, and was living in a hostel in the City of London. He was found passed out in the street within one of the police cordons, and died on his way to hospital. The police released a statement saying that he had been found not breathing, that the police had come under attack with bottles while they were trying to help, and that the man had died, a story that was then reported by the *Evening Standard* as "Police pelted with bricks as they help dying man".[64]

It wasn't long before this story began to unravel, partly due to the work of reporters like the *Guardian*'s Paul Lewis, but also due to moments of sheer chance, such as an American banker realising that he had filmed Tomlinson shortly before he died. Gradually, more information began to come in — eyewitnesses had seen Tomlinson being pushed to the ground by a police officer while he had his back turned, an event that gradually became clear through the revelation of various moments of footage. The initial post-mortem came to the conclusion that Tomlinson had died from coronary artery disease, with no evidence of any assault, yet a second autopsy — after his contact with police was revealed — actually came to the conclusion that he died from internal bleeding caused by blunt-force trauma to the abdomen. The significance of the autopsy reports was that the first one was conducted under the auspices of the City of London Police, who were effectively investigating themselves (the pathologist who conducted the first autopsy was struck off a few years later for a number of professional blunders of this sort).

Slowly the picture became clearer — Tomlinson had been trying to make his way home, but had repeatedly run up against cordons and blockages as the police were clearing the area of demonstrators. He had already been bitten by a police dog a little earlier when he was struck by a baton on the back of the legs and then pushed to the ground. He got up, remonstrated with the officers involved, walked off, but collapsed a few minutes later. He was attended to by protestors, who called the ambulance, while the police were seen to not be helping at all. The shower of bricks that the police had implied turned out to be one plastic bottle thrown at them. Unaware of the emergency on the ground, the thrower was swiftly reprimanded by other protestors.

The officer who had knocked Tomlinson to the ground, Simon Harwood, was a member of the Territorial Support Group, and who, it later turned out, had a history of being reported for violence, at one point even resigning from the force to avoid prosecution, only to find his way back through a desk job at another force. He was eventually tried for manslaughter but was found not guilty, although he was dismissed from the force afterwards.

The death of Tomlinson was a tragedy that brought to light a number of factors: one, the aggression that the police and security services brought with them to the policing of protest, which may have been thought to have lain in the bad old days; and two, the closing of ranks that occurred, whereby the sympathetic press parroted a line fed to them by the police, who were aware of what had happened but hoped that they could effectively get away with it. The investigation laid bare old practices of hiring dubious professionals who mysteriously come up with convenient scientific results, and of using retirement and resignation as a way to avoid embarrassing disciplinary action against the police. Again, this was all well-known police behaviour, but one might have thought it belonged to a previous era.

How did Johnson respond to all this? In an interview on the radio after the revelations of what actually happened to Tomlinson came out, Johnson said: "I worry that there are large sections of the media that are currently engaged in a very unbalanced orgy of cop bashing."[65] The point was that they were only doing their job after all, and the vast majority of people got home safely in the end, didn't they? This was the first example of how Johnson's approach to issues of violence and civil disorder would pan out — a swift reversion to authoritarian cliché. There would be a number of further examples of public disorder and police brutality before his term was out, and in each case Johnson either failed to assert control, sided with the guilty party, or even made matters worse. It was in this realm that his lack of seriousness had its worst consequences, at least until the year that followed his departure.

#

The next year saw a further wave of unrest in London, mainly as a result of the publication of the Browne Report into higher-education funding, and the subsequent decision to raise tuition fees to £9,000 a year. This, alongside the removal of the Education Maintenance Allowance (EMA), which was allowing many younger working-class people to attend college, led to an outpouring of energy from a younger generation and led to some of the most significant protests in the UK since the anti-war movement in 2003. Over the course of the period between October 2010 and March 2011, the students came out on the streets on a number of occasions, mainly in protests in Central London that were marked by a number of memorable and infamous events.

The first major protest was on 10th November 2010, called by the National Union of Students, and drawing tens of thousands down to the area around Parliament. Perhaps slightly cowed in the aftermath of the Tomlinson affair, perhaps because of the young age of most of the protesters, or perhaps for other reasons, the police took a surprisingly low profile at this demonstration. It seems rather foolish in retrospect, but the march was allowed to pass by Millbank Tower where the Conservative

Party have their campaign headquarters, and it was at this march that the press were given another round of photogenic destruction, as marchers broke into the building and occupied it.

It took the police hours to regain control of Millbank, and in that time there were scenes of fire extinguishers being thrown from the roof, and other symbolic carnage. The police claimed afterwards that they were unprepared for this event, and the embarrassment of having one of their own buildings trashed must have been utterly galling for the Conservatives, with David Cameron saying that he "was worried for the safety of people in the building because I know people who work in there".[66] Johnson continued his authoritarian lurch with a fairly standard "This is intolerable and all those involved will be pursued and they will face the full force of the law".[67]

The next major student demonstration took place later that month on 24th November, with the police turning up in far greater numbers, and protestors breaking off and moving quickly around the city, looking to avoid being caught up in what were now becoming the inevitable "kettles", a situation that happened again at a demonstration on 30th November. The energy of the protests was remarkable, inflamed by the specific injustice of the situation but also as one part of what was unfolding elsewhere in the world, as that winter saw the beginning of the Arab Spring, a global situation encapsulated in the title of Paul Mason's book *Why It's Kicking Off Everywhere*.

Around this time many of the universities became the site of occupations, in a kind of rerun of the post-1968 era, grabbing hold of institutional spaces as an attempt to create fragments of alternative worlds. I visited one of the occupations at the time, watched as the students sat with their laptops, engaging in meetings about social-media strategy, using that peculiar shaky-hands method of consensus decision-making. I was roped into sitting on a panel and talking about architecture and politics, a discussion which at one point was interrupted by a student — now a prominent figure in radical left-wing media — telling us to "Stop talking about utopia, don't you understand? We're actually living it!"

Looking back, after a gap of now nearly a decade, in which the energy has almost completely dissipated, a cynical look at those events does in some ways suggest that the main thing to have been achieved by the protests of that era was a generation of ambitious young journalists getting their first scoops through breathless reportage on doe-eyed young students in hoodies, shaking as they tried to light their cigarettes in the cold. This is not to say that at the time it seemed like a revolution might actually be happening, but it is galling to see how little effort it took the establishment to absorb most of these energies.

The 9th of December 2010 saw another protest, on the day of the Parliament vote on the education bill, where things nearly reached the point of disaster. Again the focus was Central London, and in this instance the memorable media shot was of the privately educated son of Pink Floyd guitarist David Gilmore swinging from the cenotaph on Whitehall, an almost sacrilegious act that landed him with a jail sentence. Elsewhere, Prince Charles and Camilla, Duchess of Cornwall, were being driven on their way to a Royal Variety performance when they became caught up in a crowd of protesters, a blurry photograph of their shocked expressions becoming a source of farcical schadenfreude in the midst of all the chaos.

Elsewhere that day, a young protester was nearly killed after being hit on the head by a police truncheon. He suffered swelling on the brain and needed emergency surgery to save his life, still carrying the scar to this day. In the aftermath, the Independent Police Complaints Commission began an investigation, but this was put on hold after the police themselves brought charges against the student for violent disorder. This began a lengthy ordeal, lasting over three separate trials, before he and a number of other students charged alongside him were unanimously found not guilty.

Towards the end of the evening of 9th December, a "kettle" was formed at Parliament Square, which was then moved slowly down to Westminster Bridge, where it was again held for a number of hours in the freezing cold. Reports from this stage of the evening suggest that the police nearly caused a genuine disaster, as the tightness of the space that the protestors were forced into on the bridge was beginning to cause severe crushing, with people on the brink of throwing themselves into the freezing river to escape.

Within a few months, the police went from having been caught completely unawares by the activities of the students, to having been on the verge of causing a large number of deaths. While the establishment and the media did their best to demonise the students, the sheer amount of evidence of violent behaviour from the state was, or should have been, shocking. This was best encapsulated by the rare conviction, five years later, of a policeman who had smashed a protestor's tooth in an unprovoked attack on the day. A recording device that the policeman thought wasn't functional picked up his comments such as "I'm gonna kill this little lot" or "I'll fucking let some people have it as well," before he discussed with his colleagues what to "nick" the student he'd just assaulted for.[68]

One remarkable aspect to all this is that there was barely a peep from Johnson throughout this whole period, except in general to condemn the negative media attention on the police, negative attention that was coming mainly from the withered left-wing of the media, which after all makes up only a few of the newspapers remaining on the stands. At the time of the G20, Johnson had been chair of the Metropolitan Police Authority, a position that made him ultimately responsible for their behaviour, but he had stood down from this in January 2010 in favour of his deputy Kit Malthouse. It would seem that Johnson was doing the usual thing and making his excuses whenever there was a political price to be paid for something, and that wading too deep into public sentiment, broadly anti-protest but also at that point sympathetic to the demands and grievances of the protestors, wasn't going to help him in the longer term.

#

Even with all the caveats regarding methodologies of collection, Johnson inherited crime statistics that were going down, and they continued to go down over his mayoralty. It seemed that the days of "no-go" estates, of horrible events like the Damilola Taylor murder in 2000, might be gone. The drug epidemics that had decimated communities were more stable than previously, and gang-related violence was not as prevalent as it had been.

But this wasn't enough really. In the last years of Livingstone's mayorship there was an abnormally high number of stabbing incidents, with twenty-seven teenagers murdered by other young people, which the press had reported as an epidemic. Johnson's 2008 manifesto naturally used the political capital attached to that, even alluding to crimes not counted in the statistics when he wrote "And we all know that we are suffering from an epidemic of unreported crime".[69] The numbers Johnson used for his claim that crime had risen went back to 1999, which masked an initial spike followed by a decline in the Livingstone years, but made for a good line in the manifesto.

What was more significant for Johnson and his relationship with the Metropolitan Police were a number of political incidents, the first of which was the ousting of Ian Blair as the Met Police Commissioner. Blair was unpopular due to his involvement in the shooting of Jean Charles de Menezes, and the campaign of misinformation afterwards, and his advocacy for draconian detention measures had not won him any friends. But he was also seen as a significant member of the New Labour establishment, with close connections with Tony Blair, and Johnson, along with Kit Malthouse, made it very clear that Blair did not have their support, and he resigned within a few months of Johnson taking office.

But almost immediately Johnson was involved in perhaps the one scandal that could have properly derailed him, after his Conservative colleague Damian Green was arrested in November 2008. The suspicion was that Green had been involved in leaking various documents from Labour's Home Office that were embarrassing to the government. Johnson managed to get himself stickily involved in the situation when it was revealed that not only had he spoken with David Cameron during a period of time when Johnson knew the arrest was about to occur, but also that he had spoken with his friend Green immediately after the arrest. In both cases Johnson denied passing any sensitive information about the investigation whatsoever over to either of his colleagues.

While it seems clear that this episode was part of the struggles of the Labour government on its last legs, limping towards its eventual defeat in 2010, and lashing out against its opponents, and while there were no charges brought in the end, it also shows Johnson at his most slippery and evasive. Completely prepared to ignore rules in the service of himself and allies, and in possession of the most cavalier attitude to truth, when the bumble wasn't carrying the day Johnson revealed himself, as in the screaming telephone call reported after he was challenged by Keith Vaz in a home affairs committee.[70]

Johnson didn't have much luck with knife crime either. Violence between young men, often gang-related, continued to flare up. The news was regularly peppered with CCTV footage showing how easily lives could be thrown away, and stories of boys being knifed for nothing more than crossing an imaginary boundary between territories continued to appear. Johnson widely promoted various different schemes to reduce the number of knives and weapons on the streets, but it seemed to make very little impact.

But these persistent criminal problems brought one particular practice into sharp relief: Stop and Search. Because if the police reaction to the protests of 2010 brought home to the students just who the police are protecting much of the time, this was never news to the many thousands of people stopped and searched by the police every year. This policy, especially its "Section 60" variation that doesn't require suspicion of an offence to take place, is widely seen as a form of racial discrimination, as it is far more likely to be enacted on young black men than any other section of the population. In London, with its long history of antagonism between the police and ethnic minorities, with the Brixton and Broadwater Farm riots, with the murder of Stephen Lawrence and the Macpherson Report, Stop and Search has long been seen as one of the main barriers between minority communities and law enforcement, and thus in many ways the state in general.

Johnson's first attempt to make a difference to the issue of knife crime in London was to, with Ian Blair still in position, set up "Blunt 2", a long-term police operation to reduce the number of knives on the streets. One of the main aspects of Operation Blunt 2 was a deliberate increase in Stop and Search, in particular to target people suspected of being in possession of knives. Over the next few years there was a massive increase in the use of the tactic, and the Met Police spoke with confidence of the numbers of weapons taken off the streets. But deaths through stabbings remained high, and the statistics didn't show with any confidence whether the tactic was working or not, as crime rose and fell in different areas seemingly regardless of how many extra searches were taking place.

In the years after the terror attacks of 2005 there had been a great institutional appetite for enhanced police powers to detain and question suspects, and the public had understandably been mostly acquiescent on that front. But in mid-2011, with the recent student unrest still a vivid memory, London was about to be pulled apart in another, shockingly familiar way.

#

On 4th August 2011, a car full of armed policemen performed a hard stop on a minicab travelling through Tottenham in Northeast London. Within a few seconds of the vehicles coming to rest, a twenty-nine-year-old man called Mark Duggan, who had been a passenger in the cab, had been shot twice and was lying dead on the ground. This was only one of a long line of deaths of black men who come into contact with the police in London, but over the next few days it would start a chain of events that would lead to the most significant civil unrest in the UK for decades. As with the deaths of de Menezes and Tomlinson, the police appeared to leak confusing information to the press in order to cloud the circumstances of what had happened, thus making it very difficult to hold them accountable for the use of deadly force, but also opening the door for all kinds of accusations of falsification, planted evidence, even extra-judicial execution.

It took the police more than a day to tell Duggan's family what had occurred, and initial media reports suggested that he had shot and injured a policeman during the incident, which turned out to have been one policeman accidentally shooting another. Images from the scene were circulating online, but there was little consistent information on what happened. On 6th August, a vigil was held outside Tottenham Police Station, with relatives, friends, and members of the local community looking for answers. Rumours went round social media of a young woman injured in a scuffle with police, and the first riot began when young men came out onto the street, causing property damage and burning a bus and other vehicles. The next day saw the unrest spread around North London and also in other areas, as more and more youths came onto the streets. Shops were looted, vehicles trashed, the police were fought, and it became abundantly clear how serious the situation was.

On the Monday, I was working from home, at my desk in a basement flat in Hackney where I lived at that point. Opening the news online, the BBC's coverage of the riots mentioned that they were spreading to numerous areas of the capital, including where I lived. I switched to the live coverage, and to my shock I saw a helicopter view of the streets outside my house, as large numbers of young men flowed across the streets, grabbing objects to hand (someone seemed to have picked up a bag of thin wooden poles) and using them to attack cars and vans that were stranded in the snarled-up traffic, before scattering off again into side streets. I opened the window to my room, which was at the back of the house, looking up into a patch of sky with no street visible, and the sound of all the different helicopters currently in the air above was ferociously loud.

There was something highly unnerving about seeing such chaos happening right outside my house, but only seeing it online. But when the helicopters seemed to be moving on, I decided to step out, and found the street outside filled with people. Some were neighbours I recognised, some were the same sort of people I saw day-to-day, but some were immediately unsettling characters, men clearly in their thirties but dressed like seventeen-year-olds with something to prove, and intently scoping out the riot police who were closing off the road at its end.

Approaching the police line, there were smashed bricks and other objects littering the street, and looking

Riot Police on the streets of Hackney, August 2011. (Image author's own).

along the street, smoke was wafting from one of the nearby streets, smoke which later turned out to have come from the single expensive red convertible sports car to be found in the area at the time, which had been torched. There was little to see, apart from the spectacle of police vans everywhere and police in full riot gear standing motionless in the street outside the house. I went back inside. Later that evening some of the most lasting images of the riots were generated: a furniture warehouse in Croydon completely ablaze, a view of a masked youth in a tracksuit in front of a burning car in Hackney, a woman remonstrating with the youths for destroying their own neighbourhoods.

The next day I was back in the office, and things were beginning to cool down, at least around where I lived, although the rioting was still significant in other parts of the country. I walked home, the weather still warm and pleasant, and as I walked north through Hackney I witnessed an incredibly telling scene. In response to the violence, various businesses had taken measures of different kinds to secure themselves. The pubs that lined the route home had the usual outside drinkers sitting on the benches, but some had attached large plywood panels to their windows, shrouding the interiors in darkness. A little further on, an upmarket coffee shop and delicatessen was completely closed off, while the premises that had taken the most effort to hide themselves away, with boards and gratings, were of course the estate agents.

In the days following the riots the writer James Meek wrote a blog post for the *London Review of Books*, describing similar scenes on the very same street,

Broadway Market: "one of the poles towards which the compass needles of estate agents and fashion-conscious yuppie couples quiver."[71] Meek described a situation he had witnessed sitting outside the coffee shop that had been boarded up, where in full view of all the trendy couples buying flat whites and sourdough bread he saw two gangs of teenagers square up to each other, scattering when one side revealed they had a gun. Meek's argument was that this displayed the urban truth behind the riots:

> This is the reality of multicultural London. It is not a melting pot. It is a set of groups that are rigidly self-separated by race, language, religion, class, money, education and age group, who have not only come to an unspoken agreement that they will not mix, but have become complacent that this agreement will not and need not be challenged.

So in amongst all this chaos, where was Johnson? Well, on holiday in Canada, as it happens. The rioting occurred when he, David Cameron, George Osborne, and Theresa May were all on summer breaks, leaving the farcical situation of Nick Clegg being the most senior politician actually in the country. Johnson initially refused to return from his break, saying "I am not going to come back at the moment because I have complete confidence in the police and I think that they are doing a very, very good job",[72] a typically flat attempt to make a situation go away. This decision not to come back was widely criticised, and by the evening of the third day of rioting he belatedly announced that he was returning.

Johnson's first appearance upon his return was at Clapham Junction, at which he was initially booed[73], as angry residents challenged him on his lacklustre response. He appeared ruffled and somewhat out of his depth, but made an attempt at a rescue in the usual fashion, by looking for a quick self-deprecating photo op, one which he found in the shape of a broom.

This broom didn't happen to be just hanging around. As the riots were unfolding, a group of horrified Londoners started a conversation on Twitter that coalesced under the name "riotcleanup". At the sight of all the destruction going on, they decided that as soon as it was safe, they would head out onto the streets to clean them up, and lo and behold, many hundreds of people did so across various parts of the city. This made for great headlines, a show of solidarity between Londoners, and lots of photographs for the media of people in marigolds sweeping away the broken glass.

Walking round Clapham, Johnson was met with shouts of "Where's your broom?", at which point he duly grabbed one, to cheers.[74] The phrase "mop-headed" may well have run through his mind at that point, and the image was duly sealed of the silly old Mayor, leading a crusade of concerned citizens against the nihilists of the night before. But of course, this kind of thing is exactly the sort of response you would expect from the world described by Meek; the comfortable majority immediately enforcing the boundary between them, the *real* citizens, and the barbarians who tore apart their own recession-hit communities. The rift displayed by the 900,000 people who joined a Facebook group supporting the Met police[75] was given visual form by the middle classes reclaiming *their* streets, through the symbolic performance of a job that other people are genuinely paid to do anyway.

The sinister character of Johnson's cuddly broom performance wasn't lost on everyone, as the performative character of the cleanup, its tweeness but also its assertion of various claims upon public space, encouraged some to go as far as to tie it into an ongoing critique of the then-swelling mix of repression and nostalgic aesthetics that was sweeping through the UK. This was the kind of cultural condition previously identified by Owen Hatherley as "ironic authoritarianism"[76], the quintessentially English masochistic taste for disciplinarian politics delivered with a queasy jolliness.

The riots were quite clearly caused by a number of factors all happening together in various degrees — distrust of police, racism, poverty and deprivation, desperation at lack of opportunities, criminality, opportunism, acquisitiveness, the sense of a carnival atmosphere, the power of momentarily taking control of spaces that are made for other people. But it became open season for people to have their own ridiculous theories. Within a few days of the initial riots the far-right, at that point mainly manifested by the English Defence League, were sending their thugs onto the streets looking for a bit of vigilante action. Elsewhere, right-wing historian David Starkey made a fool out of himself by going on the news and claiming that "the whites have become black" through listening to too much rap music.

Even the architecture world wasn't above making their own sweeping generalisations, after respected consultancy Space Syntax, who earn much of their money from providing reports on the legibility of street layouts in proposed new developments, swiftly published a press release that claimed that, seeing as the majority of convicted rioters came from post-war council estates, there had to be something wrong with the *design* of said estates[77], that just maybe the commercial services offered by Space Syntax might be able to help with. Thankfully this kind of disingenuous tosh, straight from the Create Streets mould, was widely ridiculed.

The Tory establishment reacted as you might imagine. David Cameron described the riots as "criminality, pure and simple"[78], which set the general tone for much of what would follow, with custodial sentences imposed upon young people just for handling clothes that had been stolen in the looting[79], which inevitably has to be compared to the total inability of the state to bring anyone to justice for the many hundreds of people who have died at the hands of the police over the last half-century.

Johnson himself started off by condemning the riots simply and emphatically, but struck a fairly measured tone in the days after, saying "I do not think that this is a simple issue, and I do not think we can simply ascribe it to wanton criminality or simply ascribe it to 'Tory cuts'".[80] But in time, Johnson, in league with Kit Malthouse and after requests from the Metropolitan police, decided that it was appropriate for London to have recourse to water cannons, a riot-control technology used on the continent, and famous for its use in Northern Ireland during the Troubles, but never before used on the British mainland.

This authoritarian gesture was immediately controversial, with images of a German man with his eyes running down his face after being hit by a water cannon at an environmentalist protest a particularly horrendous symbol. Objections ranged from the principled — that it was a shocking escalation of the powers of the civil authority, a gross violation of human rights — to the tactical — that it's only really useful when used to disperse a static wall of protesters, rather than a fast-moving network of small groups.

Johnson went ahead and purchased three second-hand water-cannon vehicles from Germany, but was unable to do anything with them, as then-Home Secretary Theresa May in the end ruled that they could not be used on the British mainland. In the end, there was no event of unrest that the cannons could even have been deployed at over the remaining years of his mayorship, and after Johnson left they were quickly sold off. But by sticking to his position over the water cannon, Johnson threw his lot in with the authoritarian tendency rather than the latent bohemianism of his background, and effectively gave up on being a unifying force in the city.

And while there was no significant repeat unrest, not during the Olympics, and not for the years afterwards, by claiming and then shirking responsibility over policing, and through the fact of his occasionally thoughtful statements on difficult situations becoming overwhelmed by his latching onto cheap soundbites and regressive tough-guy statements and policies, Johnson completely failed to achieve anything even remotely significant in terms of symbolically improving relationships between communities and the police, or indeed communities and each other.

In early 2016 Johnson reprised his broom moment when he joined in with "Clean for the Queen", a ludicrous campaign set up for her majesty's 90th birthday by Keep Britain Tidy, seemingly taking the concept of "ironic authoritarianism" as an aspiration. There he was, stuffed into an undersized purple jumper along with Michael Gove and other politicians, stood in front of a display clearly derived from the ubiquitous Keep Calm and Carry On poster, looking studiously ludicrous as ever. It was one of the last appearances he made as Mayor, having already become an MP again in the safe Tory seat of Uxbridge and South Ruislip at the 2015 general election, a move that everyone assumed was the next step on his journey to being PM.

CONCLUSION

"I enjoyed it hugely;
it was a massive privilege"

Boris Johnson, Prime Minister?

It all happened very quickly. There he was, at the lectern, the usual smirk and sparkle still there but decidedly dulled. His statement began with some mock Classical rhetoric, borrowed from Shakespeare's *Julius Caesar*: "It is a time not to fight against the tide of history, but to take that tide at the flood, and sail on to fortune", he mumbled, the words falling out of his mouth reluctantly, as if they preferred it back there in his throat. He continued in this vein for nearly a quarter of an hour, cliché after cliché about sovereignty, greatness, about paying attention to those left behind by society. It was statesmanlike, for sure, but it lacked the vim and gusto that we've come to expect.

He listed a series of his achievements at City Hall, his claim to have lowered the crime rate, to have done his best to enable the fulfilment of the poorest in society. He claimed that when he left office there were 40,000 sites under development, and over 100,000 housing units built, and told those watching that when he had taken power, London was home to four of the six poorest boroughs in the country, but was now home to none of the poorest twenty. "The prophets of doom were wrong then, and they are wrong now", he forced out of himself.

Then, after a run-through of the challenges that were facing the country after the EU Referendum, he brought his monologue to a close:

> That is the agenda for the next Prime Minister of this country. Well, I must tell you, my friends, you who have waited faithfully for the punchline of this speech, that having consulted colleagues and in view of the circumstances in Parliament, I have concluded that person cannot be me.[81]

And that was that.

This press conference was supposed to have been the announcement of Johnson's campaign for Prime Minister, the culmination of a lifetime's ambition, which every action of his had been leading to for almost the entire last fifty-two years. Only a few days before, David Cameron had marched out to another lectern set up on Downing Street and announced his resignation, bringing to an end what must surely go down as one of the most pathetic premierships in British history, brought low as the result of a gamble that he believed was a sure way to reign in the more head-banging tendency in his party once and for all. Off back into No. 10 he strode, whistling a jaunty tune, to languish forever in historic ridicule.

But now, his arch nemesis Johnson was walking away too, stabbed in the back by colleagues, hence the Caesar reference in the speech. At nine a.m. that day, 30th June 2016, Michael Gove, who had been lined up for the chancellor's job under Johnson, announced that he was running too. Johnson immediately recognised that his necessary support was gone, and rather than lose the race, he dropped out, his one and only dream evaporating before him.

A friend of mine once suggested that Johnson was a sufferer of what they ironically called "the curse of the public schoolboy": that no matter how little effort they put in, no matter how little aptitude for something they have, they cannot help but succeed anyway. Sonia Purnell's 2011 book *Just Boris* claimed that Johnson's mayoral candidacy was just a ruse on his way to the PM job, stating it was "Quite likely he subscribed to the widely held opinion that it was impossible he could win, but had gambled that a narrow, yet glorious defeat might be just the career booster needed".[82] Well now it had happened again, this time as tragedy following farce: it was widely believed that Johnson only joined the campaign to leave the EU as a strategy to raise his profile for a leadership bid, expecting, like Cameron, that it would be an easy loss. But now they'd won, the fires of xenophobia had been thoroughly stoked, and the UK was driving itself off a cliff.

A few weeks later, on the 15th of July, the staff of the estate agent Foxtons in Islington were told to stop work early. A demo had been called by the anarchist group Class War, a fixture on the fringes of the left in various forms since the early 1980s, fondly known for their dark humour and recuperation of tabloid rhetoric. The demo was to take place outside Johnson's house, where the protesters planned to chant "Liar Liar Pants on Fire" and symbolically defenestrate an effigy. Foxtons estate agents are often the focus of anti-gentrification protests, so they worried that if the protestors came anywhere near them they might be a target.

Outside Johnson's house, the police were containing a small, vocal, but generally good natured protest, including young anarchists masked up and in all black, and various older stalwarts of the movement. But then the journalists who were there witnessed an incredible scene. Some blue-suited lads from the Foxtons office, who had clearly been in the pub all afternoon, came swaggering down the road yelling "OH BORIS I LOVE YOU!" before wading right into the protest, which duly kicked off. The estate agents brawled with the anarchists, and then had to be pulled away by the police. In the process a sixty-five-year-old woman was knocked to the ground suffering a neck injury, there were a number of scuffles, and protestors let off flares before the police asserted order.

When footage of the fight made the news Foxtons duly sacked the estate agents, and three men were charged, two with assaulting the police, although charges were later dropped. But what a scene, a preposterous satire of the historic moment. Foxtons are well known as the most visible, most rapacious, and most despised estate agents in London, which is saying something when you consider how highly estate agents are regarded in general. And here they were, keepers of the housing crisis turned foot soldiers for Brexit-delivering Johnson.

But this was just how 2016 seemed to go. I was already working on this book at the point of the EU Referendum, and I had the sudden rather perturbing thought that it might be finished in a country where its subject had become the Prime Minister, a country moreover on a steep slope towards a form of chaos, with the right-wing press screaming about "Enemies of the People", with politicians being murdered in the street, and forces of racism and intolerance emboldened by the dynamics that had been unleashed. I don't suppose for a second that Johnson won't be back, won't eventually get his chance, but for now the prospect seems to have passed, as he has been kept on as Foreign Secretary by the new Prime Minister Theresa May, surely at least partly as a humiliation.

The other effect of the developments of the last year is an apparent lessening of the gravity of his previous offences. For what is the commissioning of a stupid and expensive piece of public art compared to, say, the prospect of people who have lived in London for many years and have built their lives here, being forced to leave the country due to tit-for-tat punishments over the EU withdrawal process? Or, for that matter, the prospect of whatever carnage seems to be unfurling from across the Atlantic?

But in a way, the story of Johnson's career is a symbol of this new world. Of course he is from the ultra-elite, the sort of person who for centuries has been able to set their sights on the top table at government and have a reasonably high expectation that they'd achieve it, the sort of person who could treat the public as so much fodder for their own desires. But the peculiarities of Johnson's personality — the flightiness, the lack of concentration, the inability to properly pretend that he's in it for any notion of public service, the spiralling rise through appearances on popular media, not to mention the ability to behave in ways that the spin-and-message-obsessed period he came up in couldn't allow — it all appears, from today's standpoint, to be exactly the kind of shallow celebrity personality that can navigate the political world with apparent nonchalance, one who is loved by exactly the sort of people they hold in least regard.

This raises a question, however. Is it the case that these negative aspects of Johnson's personality are intrinsically linked to his ability to make things happen? Can we even imagine a character like Johnson being able to concentrate their considerable power on less frivolous and more beneficial projects? Perhaps this is an oxymoronic question, as surely much of Johnson's power comes from the ongoing dialectical spin between on the one hand his intellect and cunning, and on the other his shallowness and lack of seriousness. It's almost inconceivable that a character like Johnson would have been able to convince a billionaire to spend hundreds of millions on, say, repairing a dilapidated housing estate, and it's not necessarily entirely his failing.

Johnson was replaced in the Mayor's chair by Sadiq Khan, the Labour candidate, after a rather unpleasant campaign by Zac Goldsmith. Led by Lynton Crosby (of course), Goldsmith's campaign traded on xenophobic and islamophobic innuendo, which thankfully and graciously fell on completely deaf London ears. Khan now finds himself perhaps the most powerful Labour politician in the country, as at the time of writing Jeremy Corbyn's leadership seems to be looking ever more likely to fizzle out miserably, as even those of us who have been most enthusiastic about his leftward turn grow weary of his and his team's failure to make an impact.

Khan has made some positive noises, including what seems like a serious commitment to increasing the number of affordable housing units, and strong words on shedding light on the scandal of developers' viability assessments. His Deputy Mayor for Planning is Jules Pipe, replacing Ed Lister who was in that role under Johnson. Pipe was previously the Labour Mayor of Hackney from 2002, and oversaw a remarkable transformation of the neighbourhood as it incorporated a massive increase in wealthier inhabitants, and a process of "regeneration" that was not always uncontroversial. Noises coming from the vicinity of City Hall suggest that even at this early stage the mood in the planning department is positive, and that there are hopes for a more sophisticated approach than the "build anything anywhere" of the last decade.

Thankfully, after a long period where he appeared to refuse a commitment either way, Khan did the right thing regarding the Garden Bridge. Without blatantly and full-heartedly dismissing the project, he commissioned a report from Dame Margaret Hodge — who in a previous life had been the Labour culture minister at the point Johnson became mayor — into the value for money of the public contribution to the scheme. Hodge's report, with which Johnson conspicuously refused to cooperate, was delivered in April 2017 and made for fine reading. Inside, Hodge detailed questionable business cases, undocumented meetings, destroyed notes, skewed and unfair tendering practices, everyone blaming everyone else (and claiming that nothing was their responsibility), and a construction contract that hooked the public purse to millions of pounds of obligations when the funds were nowhere near in place. And looming over it all was a sense of thunderous pressure coming from Johnson himself, trying to force the bridge to the point of no return before the electoral cycle came round again.

The report was extremely damning, with an understated viciousness that only English legalese can really achieve. Some particularly choice moments included remarks on how both Richard Di Cani and Isabel Dedring (Johnson's Deputy Mayor for Transport) had — after dubiously awarding them the contract — subsequently taken jobs at Arup, and how the only public supporters of the bridge appeared to be The Garden Bridge Trust, *The Evening Standard* and Johnson himself. After publication, Khan spent a week or so holding on in rather delicious suspense, and then confirmed that he would not guarantee any funds for construction to begin. Now, unless an ultra-high-net-worth-individual comes along with a solid gold offer, the Garden Bridge is cancelled.

But with Khan, much also hinges on what happens on a national level. The possibility is that "Brexit" will lead to a determined regulatory effort on the part of the EU to remove the local advantages of the City of London, and there is a chance that many businesses might leave the capital, removing much of its financial power. This might have ameliorating effects on housing costs for ordinary people, but might also mean a collapse in the office market, and knock-on collapses in other parts of the economy of the city, most conspicuously leisure. But on the other hand, Brexit could also lead to an even less regulated environment, where London becomes effectively a tax haven, which would serve to inflate living costs even more, and stretch inequality yet further still. In the near-total uncertainty of the current period, both of these possibilities are believable.

But how else could Johnson have been? His close counterpart in New York, Michael Bloomberg, overseer of the hyper-gentrification of Manhattan, was replaced in 2013 by Bill de Blasio, who ran on a campaign that vowed to combat the excesses of the NYPD's "stop and frisk" policies, and also to tackle the city's housing crisis, two factors that could easily have been attractive parts of Khan's campaign in London. But a useful comparison to be made is with Paris: a city whose geographical wealth gap has often been cited as the end destination for the housing crisis of London, with its shining wealthy core and its poor concentrated outside the Périphérique.

But over the same period as the Johnson years, the Mayor of Paris — first Bertrand Delanoë and since 2015 Anne Hidalgo — and the Parisian authorities have made great efforts to increase not just the supply of "affordable" homes at a proportion of market rent, but genuinely social homes owned by the state. Throughout the Johnson years, Paris was building around 6,000 socially rented homes per year[83], at subsidised rates of less than fifty percent of what the market charges. Furthermore, the housing that is constructed in Paris is frequently designed by talented architects, and often located in areas dominated by wealthier housing, a strategy of deliberate social mixing that hasn't been seen in London since the radical councils of the late 1960s. It may not be enough to overcome the crisis, but it would not have been impossible in London with the right kind of political support.

Even more radical options are also possible. The Mayor of Barcelona since 2015 has been Ada Colau. Affiliated with no major party, she rose to prominence as a leading member of a group campaigning for mortgage justice after the 2009 financial crisis, due to the number of repossessions and evictions that were going on. After five years of demonstrations and campaigns, including a number of arrests, she ran for Mayor under a new political platform, and won a majority, with a radical agenda for housing and economic justice. On a recent visit to the city the sense of excitement (admittedly from left-wing architects) regarding her leadership was infectious. This is not to say that this could easily have happened in London — the contours of the crisis have been very different, and the financial industry has a power that is unfathomable — but it shows, to resort to cliché, that another world is possible.

In the last instance the Mayor of London does not have a great deal of power, and perhaps it is too much to suggest that in the wider context the Mayor of one city could have done all that much to deal with many issues that relate directly to the workings of the global economy. And the terrible imbalance between the economy of London and the wider UK, which clearly played such a huge factor in the lead-up to the Brexit vote, is the result of decades of neglect and often deliberately imposed decline, and is something that the Mayor could have little effect upon.

There is another argument, however, that the ongoing crisis of the nation state, of which regressive nationalism is just yet another symptom, might lead to a renewed importance for the city as a specific political entity, one capable of coordinating policies and initiatives in a more democratic way, both within its own population but also in collaboration with other cities. In a scenario like that, the Mayor becomes a far more powerful figure, and in the short term and within the UK at least, this scenario is being borne out by the creation of a number of new mayoralties, and a renewed interest from politicians in taking up those positions.

Perhaps the period 2008–16 will one day be looked at as a lucky break for London, without major catastrophe, and with an economy that was relatively robust throughout all the other turmoil that was going on. People may look back at some of the prominent architecture and design from that period, and see in it an innocence that was almost endearing. But it's just as likely that the architecture of the Johnson years will be seen as quintessentially vulgar, with an almost prelapsarian quality, the trinkets and towers of the last moments before things went very wrong. The answer is no doubt somewhere in-between, but looking back from this point, perhaps the least we could hope for is that someone in a position like that might have taken their job just that little bit more seriously.

Acknowledgements

Thanks are due to Tariq, Tamar, Josh, Johnny and all at Repeater.

There are numerous people whose own work on Johnson's impact on the built environment of London has been vital, some of whom I have engaged in fruitful discussion during the production of *Nincompoopolis*. These include Alberto Duman, Dawn Foster, Dan Hancox, Owen Hatherley, Oliver Wainwright, and others.

All of the text is original, although various sections of *Nincompoopolis* draw on previous writing or speaking engagements that have appeared in *Bauwelt*, *Frieze* magazine, *The Guardian*, *Icon Magazine*, *The New Statesman*, *The Information Project*, The Mackintosh School of Architecture, and others.

Thanks to the various employers who make this kind of work feasible, including Lynch Architects, Royal College of Art, Central St. Martins and many others.

Thanks to Marin Tamm, who makes anything possible.

Two people who were influential on this book but who are no longer with us are Mark Fisher, without whose encouragement I would never have begun writing critically, and Tom Barry, who I never physically met, but whose 'Boriswatch' alias online kept an extremely funny but entirely serious eye on Johnson's antics, and with whom I had many enlightening conversations. This book is dedicated to them.

Notes

1 http://www.newstatesman.com/politics/uk/2016/07/
boris-johnson-peddled-absurd-eu-myths-and-our-
disgraceful-press-followed-his

2 https://www.youtube.com/watch?v=iDJWkS2A9To

3 http://www.telegraph.co.uk/news/politics/london-
mayor-election/mayor-of-london/2666041/Boris-
Johnson-in-whiff-whaff-ping-pong-row.html

4 https://www.theguardian.com/sport/2011/jul/31/
london-olympics-aquatic-hadid-review

5 See Sinclair, I., "A Hit of Rus in Urbe", *London Review of
Books*, v.24, n.12, 27 June 2002.

6 "What's on — The Slide", http://arcelormittalorbit.com/
whats-on/the-slide/, accessed 22 Nov 2016.

7 http://news.bbc.co.uk/1/hi/uk_politics/1815532.stm

8 http://corporate.arcelormittal.com/who-we-are/
arcelormittal-orbit/perspectives/boris-johnson

9 https://twitter.com/ollywainwright/
status/751849272115662848, accessed 23 Nov 2016.

10 http://www.bdonline.co.uk/early-concept-sketches-of-
the-olympic-park-arcelormittal-orbit/5002566.article

11 https://www.theguardian.com/sport/2015/oct/20/
olympic-parks-orbit-tower-costing-taxpayer-10000-a-
week

12 http://www.telegraph.co.uk/news/2016/04/26/
anish-kapoor-boris-foisted-new-slide-on-my-sculpture/

13 http://news.bbc.co.uk/1/hi/uk/1098465.stm

14 See Spencer, D., *The Architecture of Neoliberalism*, London: Bloomsbury, 2016, p.133-7

15 https://www.theguardian.com/uk/2010/jul/05/thames-cable-car-plan-unveiled

16 https://www.theguardian.com/media/2012/may/02/news-international-boris-johnson-leveson

17 http://www.mayorwatch.co.uk/cable-car-sponsorship-deal-includes-anti-israel-clause/

18 https://www.theguardian.com/business/2015/jan/18/coca-cola-london-eye-charity-anger

19 http://news.bbc.co.uk/1/hi/uk_politics/7014739.stm

20 Johnson, B., "Hop on and off the bus for a ride to freedom and growth", *The Telegraph*, 19 May 2013.

21 https://insidecroydon.files.wordpress.com/2015/02/boris-to-ni-nov-2012.pdf

22 http://www.newstatesman.com/politics/2014/03/boris-johnson-s-plan-sell-public-land-new-crystal-palace-will-be-terrible

23 https://insidecroydon.com/2014/11/20/boris-signals-defeat-on-his-chinese-giveaway-at-crystal-palace/

24 https://www.theguardian.com/artanddesign/2014/jun/24/garden-bridge-london-thomas-heatherwick-joanna-lumley

25 https://www.newcivilengineer.com/joannas-ab-fab-idea/837892.article

26 http://www.fashionarchitecturetaste.com/2005/11/diana_bridge.html

27 https://www.theguardian.com/artanddesign/2015/may/24/joanna-lumley-role-boris-johnson-thames-garden-bridge-london-thomas-heatherwick

28 http://www.itv.com/news/london/2015-02-04/
handwritten-note-from-joanna-lumley-reveals-cycle-
path-in-original-garden-bridge-plans/

29 http://www.bbc.co.uk/news/
uk-england-london-35439976

30 https://www.theguardian.com/uk-news/2013/nov/14/
boris-johnson-london-cycling-deaths

31 http://www.independent.co.uk/news/uk/home-news/
bob-crow-dies-rmt-union-leader-dead-at-52-9183607.
html

32 Beckett, A., *When the Lights Went Out*, London: Faber
and Faber, 2009, p.35–46.

33 https://www.theguardian.com/politics/
davehillblog/2010/jul/19/boris-johnson-jules-pipe-
letter-duncan-smith-housing-benefit-london

34 https://www.london.gov.uk/what-we-do/planning/
planning-applications-and-decisions/public-hearings/
hertsmere-house-columbus

35 https://www.london.gov.uk/what-we-do/planning/
planning-applications-and-decisions/public-hearings/
southall-gas-works-public

36 https://www.london.gov.uk/what-we-do/planning/
planning-applications-and-decisions/public-hearings/
saatchi-block-public-hearing

37 https://www.london.gov.uk/what-we-do/planning/
planning-applications-and-decisions/public-hearings/
southwark-free-school-public

38 https://www.london.gov.uk/what-we-do/planning/
planning-applications-and-decisions/public-hearings/
alpha-square

39 https://www.london.gov.uk/what-we-do/planning/planning-applications-and-decisions/public-hearings/trocoll-house

40 https://www.london.gov.uk/what-we-do/planning/planning-applications-and-decisions/public-hearings/city-forum-250-city-road

41 https://www.london.gov.uk/what-we-do/planning/planning-applications-and-decisions/public-hearings/holy-trinity-primary-school

42 https://www.london.gov.uk/what-we-do/planning/planning-applications-and-decisions/public-hearings/eileen-house-public-hearing

43 https://www.london.gov.uk/what-we-do/planning/planning-applications-and-decisions/public-hearings/london-fruit-and-wool

44 https://www.london.gov.uk/what-we-do/planning/planning-applications-and-decisions/public-hearings/land-blossom-street

45 https://www.london.gov.uk/what-we-do/planning/planning-applications-and-decisions/public-hearings/monmouth-house-public

46 https://www.london.gov.uk/what-we-do/planning/planning-applications-and-decisions/public-hearings/convoys-wharf-public-hearing

47 https://www.london.gov.uk/what-we-do/planning/planning-applications-and-decisions/public-hearings/former-westferry-printworks

48 http://www.independent.co.uk/voices/comment/mount-unpleasant-how-the-royal-mail-group-will-make-a-fortune-from-selling-flats-to-private-9080865.html

49 Letter to Mayor's Office, 10th January 2014, https://www.london.gov.uk/what-we-do/planning/planning-applications-and-decisions/public-hearings/mount-pleasant-sorting

50 http://www.savills.co.uk/research_articles/141285/198087-0

51 http://www.peterbarberarchitects.com/coldbath-town/

52 "Building a Better London", Housing manifesto, accessed here: http://image.guardian.co.uk/sys-files/Guardian/documents/2009/04/27/borishousingmanifesto.pdf

53 https://www.london.gov.uk/what-we-do/regeneration/regeneration-publications/design-standards-new-homes-london

54 http://www.standard.co.uk/comment/simon-jenkins-only-a-new-tax-will-prevent-this-being-a-ghost-town-9214199.html

55 http://www.telegraph.co.uk/comment/columnists/borisjohnson/10456202/We-should-be-humbly-thanking-the-super-rich-not-bashing-them.html

56 http://www.bbc.co.uk/news/uk-england-london-11642662

57 http://www.bdonline.co.uk/boris-johnson-approves-heygate-demolition/5051187.article

58 http://www.cityam.com/article/1378091289/exclusive-walkie-scorchie-melted-my-jag

59 https://www.vice.com/en_us/article/dan-hancox-regeneration-supernove

60 http://www.standard.co.uk/news/politics/boris-johnson-don-t-be-afraid-of-chinese-firms-buying-into-london-8879135.html

61 https://www.channel4.com/news/boris-johnson-london-propery-deal-china-albert-dock

62 https://insidecroydon.com/2015/02/06/two-years-of-secret-meetings-for-worlds-largest-glass-house/

63 House of Lords Committee for Privileges and Conduct, "The Conduct of Lord Bates", 2015, p.5.

64 https://www.theguardian.com/uk/2009/aug/04/ian-tomlinson-death-g20

65 https://www.theguardian.com/politics/2009/apr/23/boris-johnson-g20-police-media

66 http://www.bbc.co.uk/news/uk-politics-11732264

67 http://www.bbc.co.uk/news/education-11726822

68 http://www.independent.co.uk/voices/comment/i-m-gonna-kill-this-lot-and-other-things-a-police-officer-shouldnt-be-saying-during-a-protest-10269742.html

69 http://image.guardian.co.uk/sys-files/Guardian/documents/2009/04/27/crime_manifesto_complete_final_final.pdf

70 http://news.bbc.co.uk/1/hi/uk_politics/7885610.stm

71 https://www.lrb.co.uk/blog/2011/08/09/james-meek/in-broadway-market/

72 http://metro.co.uk/2011/08/07/boris-johnson-i-wont-cut-short-my-holiday-to-deal-with-tottenham-riots-106572/

73 https://www.youtube.com/watch?v=axeCXcMG4CM

74 http://www.bbc.co.uk/news/magazine-14475741

75 http://www.dailymail.co.uk/news/article-2024358/UK-RIOTS-2011-Sikhs-defend-temple-locals-protect-pubs-Britons-defy-rioters.html

76 https://www.radicalphilosophy.com/commentary/lash-out-and-cover-up

77 http://www.spacesyntax.com/project/2011-london-riots/

78 http://www.telegraph.co.uk/news/uknews/
    crime/8691034/London-riots-Prime-Ministers-
    statement-in-full.html

79 http://www.bbc.co.uk/news/uk-14553330

80 https://www.theguardian.com/
    politics/davehillblog/2011/aug/12/
    boris-johnson-says-london-riots-not-a-simple-issue

81 https://www.youtube.com/watch?v=mzCoyAm_0Dg

82 Purnell, S., *Just Boris: A Tale of Blond Ambition*, London:
    Aurum Press, 2011, p.317.

83 http://www.insidehousing.co.uk/a-tale-of-two-
    cities/6529731.article#

Repeater Books

is dedicated to the creation of a new reality. The landscape of twenty-first-century arts and letters is faded and inert, riven by fashionable cynicism, egotistical self-reference and a nostalgia for the recent past. Repeater intends to add its voice to those movements that wish to enter history and assert control over its currents, gathering together scattered and isolated voices with those who have already called for an escape from Capitalist Realism. Our desire is to publish in every sphere and genre, combining vigorous dissent and a pragmatic willingness to succeed where messianic abstraction and quiescent co-option have stalled: abstention is not an option: we are alive and we don't agree.